ONE GOSPEL – MANY CLOTHES
Anglicans and the Decade of Evangelism

Dr John Stott

ONE GOSPEL – MANY CLOTHES
Anglicans and the Decade of Evangelism

Case-studies on evangelism to mark the retirement of John Stott as president of the Evangelical Fellowship in the Anglican Communion.

Edited by Christopher Wright
and Christopher Sugden

Published by:
The Evangelical Fellowship in the Anglican Communion (EFAC) and Regnum Books

The Evangelical Fellowship in the Anglican Communion was founded
in 1961 to foster fellowship among Anglican Evangelicals
throughout the world. It comprises 19 national fellowships. The
international co-ordinator is Bishop David Evans, assistant bishop
of Bradford, 30 Grovesnor Road, Shipley, Bradford, U.K. It
publishes a bi-annual EFAC Bulletin available from P.O. Box 70,
Oxford, U.K.

Regnum Books is a two-thirds world publishing company publishing
on behalf of the African Theological Fraternity, the Latin American
Theological Fraternity, and Partnership in Mission Asia. It works
in co-operation with major western Christian organisations and is
based at the Oxford Centre for Mission Studies, P.O.Box 70,
Oxford, U.K.

ISBN 1-870345-08-8

British Library Cataloguing in Publication Data

One gospel – many clothes : Anglicans and the decade of
    evangelism.
    1. Church of England. Evangelism
    I. Wright, Christopher *1924*– II. Sugden, Chris
    269.2

Typeset by Opus, Becket Street, Oxford
and printed by BPCC Wheatons, Ltd, Exeter
for EFAC and Regnum Books, P.O. Box 70, Oxford, U.K.

Table of Contents

Foreword

This book is dedicated to the honour of one of God's most remarkable and productive servants – Dr John Stott. When the annals are read in Heaven the effects of this one holy life will be seen in an amazing diversity of worldwide fruition for Christ and His Church.

What is so noteable that it affects all John Stott does? I suggest to you that it is his attention to the Root or Roots in order to bring sound growth. For him *the* fundamental root is his Lord, Jesus Christ – the foundation of all his thinking and living. When asked what his greatest aim is he usually replies 'to be more like Christ'.

The next stage of the rooting for him is in Scripture. As a curate I attended, by invitation, a meeting of a group of 40 clergy under the age of 40. This group was founded by John Stott when under 40 himself and was called Eclectics. It was for me a revelation, a release, a dynamic experience. Evangelicals at the time were so often controlled by 'evangelical tradition' in how to act and behave in life. There, in Eclectics, the one condition was the acceptance of the Scripture as Authority – but then everything else was to be tested in the light of Scripture. It was liberating! It was the key to evangelical revival in the Church of England. It was going back to the roots.

This book will warm John Stott's heart because it goes for the roots – and in particular the root of mission and evangelism. In the confusion (by universalists) over why there needs to be a Decade of Evangelism, it is essential to go back to the root of the theology of evangelism; in the reluctance to evangelise by the Church in general (like the Corinthians of old) it is necessary to stir it to the primacy of this task for the Church; in the danger of separating evangelism into some particular method, it is vital to see examples of incarnating it in diversely different societies and countries; and in the danger of supposing that evangelism with the Gospel can ignore the physical and social needs of people, it refreshingly underlines the great emphasis of the Lausanne Covenant on Evangelism (where John Stott was a major influence) of reaching the whole person. These are all roots for fruitful evangelism.

All over the world are flourishing Christian enterprises, groups, organisations and churches that were helped directly or indirectly by John Stott to get back to their roots or to begin from proper roots – the roots of Christ, the Word and evangelism. They have been fruitful in growth because of those roots. EFAC is one of them. We pay tribute by this volume to Dr John Stott – a man of roots and root-cultivator supreme – a man who, above everything else, pays supreme tribute to the One in Whom his own life is rooted, the Lord Jesus Christ.

Michael Baughen
Bishop of Chester
Petertide 1990

Chapter One

An Evangelical Anglican Theological Consultation

Christopher Wright and Christopher Sugden

The Lambeth Decade

At the Lambeth Conference in 1988, a process took place which placed "A Decade of Evangelism" firmly on the agenda of the Anglican Communion. The initiative came from the African bishops. The Archbishop of Canterbury had invited the bishops to "bring their dioceses with them". This meant that bishops from Africa such as Dinis Singulane from Mozambique and David Gitari from Mount Kenya East could bring their stories of evangelism and church planting under very difficult circumstances.[1] Their example became a challenge to the whole communion to make the 1990's a decade of evangelism.

The report of the Lambeth Conference *The Truth Shall Make You Free* contains a statement on Mission and Ministry that is outstanding and sets a valuable framework for understanding evangelism. It states

"Mission involves proclamation. Proclamation must proceed from a Church and a people who reflect the love and goodness of God. We are called to proclaim God's love and forgiveness by word and by deed. We must use every means available to spread the message of salvation. Our proclamation must be sensitive to the culture and beliefs of others. Nevertheless, Christ calls all people to turn from evil and all that hurts or enslaves and to receive the fullness of life which he alone can give.

The salvation we proclaim is concerned both with the wholeness of individuals and the wholeness of society. Any understanding which focuses on the individual and ignores society as a whole, or vice versa, is not true to the Gospel. Abuse or exploitation of others is contrary to God's purpose.

Part of our mission is to challenge that in society or in us which is life-denying. It is also to bring hope, love and trust, so that all are raised to the full dignity and stature of their humanity.

Evangelism is the communication of the good news of Christ's Kingdom and his accompanying command to people to repent, believe and be baptized into his Body, the Church.

Transformation is the positive action of establishing conditions where wholeness in human life may be enjoyed. . . Transformation will mean that all that demeans human dignity (e.g. discrimination on grounds of race, sex or class), or prevents access to basic community resources (e.g. medical and educational facilities), or pollutes the environment or allows natural resources to be plundered (e.g. the removal of fish by some powers in the Pacific Ocean or the removal of indigenous people from their land) is to be resisted.

Both evangelism and the transformation of society are responsibilities to be fulfilled by the whole people of God. In some cases, they will go hand in hand; the efforts for transformation will be visible expressions of the Church's concern for the total person as the evangelistic message is proclaimed and shared. On other occasions, transformation will follow as people turn to God, are incorporated into the Church, and seek, as they are taught, to witness in the world by their lifestyle as they serve their fellows, conscious of their weakness but also of the power of God." [2]

Theological Resourcing

At Lambeth many bishops from all parts of the Anglican Communion expressed an important need for sustained biblical teaching on matters of faith and conduct. In response to this, the executive committee of the Evangelical Fellowship in the Anglican Communion established a "Theological Resource Team" to address issues which required theological reflection. The executive identified that one of the important issues was the very theme of evangelism to which the bishops had committed the communion. The Theological Resource Team called a study conference to gather case studies of evangelism from all parts of the Anglican Communion and to examine the theological assumptions underlying the evangelistic practice of which they spoke.

Guidelines for Case Studies

The Guidelines for the Case Studies had been developed by C.B. Samuel, the director of the Evangelical Fellowship of India Commission on Relief and Vinay Samuel, the former general secretary of EFAC for use in the Social Concern and Evangelisation Track of the Lausanne II Congress on Evangelism at Manila in July 1989.[3] These were modified for use in Anglican contexts. Each contributor was asked to present their case study in response to the questions set out in the guidelines. Many of the contributors at the conference remarked how the guidelines had prompted them to think in greater depth about their evangelistic practice.

The case-studies were shared and discussed in depth at the conference in Mombasa. In counterpoint with that discussion there was biblical reflection on a number of passages. For instance, our discussion of evangelism to communities took place in counterpoint with our reflection on Ezekiel 18, where the prophet insists on individual responsibility before God.

Out of these discussions emerged a number of themes which the participants had a common mind about and wished to share with the wider Communion through a report. That report, *Gospel, Community and Church* is included at the end of the book.

John Stott

This volume is dedicated as a *festschrift* to John Stott, the founder and current president of EFAC on the occasion of his retirement from that post. As part of our tribute we include one of John Stott's most recent pieces, originally given as an address on the Decade of Evangelism in Melbourne, Australia in April 1990.

We are grateful to Bishop Michael Baughen for joining in this tribute.

Footnotes:

1. David Gitari and Dinis Singulane's contributions are summarised and discussed in *Lambeth: A View from the Two Thirds World* by Vinay Samuel and Christopher Sugden (London, S.P.C.K. 1989).
2. *The Truth Shall Make You Free* edited by Michael Nazir-Ali and Derek Pattinson, (Anglican Consultative Council, 1988).
3. The original guidelines are published in *Transformation* July 1990.

Chapter Two

Evangelism Through the Local Church

John Stott

We should be very grateful to the African bishops for proposing, and to the other bishops for agreeing, that the last ten years of the twentieth century, indeed of the second millenium AD, should be declared "A Decade of Evangelism".

This decision of the 1988 Lambeth Conference has brought evangelism to the top of the Anglican Church's agenda and challenges us to ask ourselves what we know and believe about evangelism. For the whole Anglican Communion now finds itself obliged to face a responsibility which it has often shirked, namely the call to bear witness to Jesus Christ.

According to the definition which the Primates have commended to us, to evangelize is 'to make known by word and deed the love of the crucified and risen Christ in the power of the Holy Spirit, so that people will repent, believe and receive Christ as their Saviour and obediently serve him as their Lord in the fellowship of his church.'

Not that evangelism is foreign to the ethos of Anglicanism. Far from it. The Second Book of Homilies, for example, written mostly by Bishop John Jewel of Salisbury, and published in 1571, contains the following admonition: 'If any man be a dumb Christian, not professing his faith openly, but cloaking and colouring himself for fear of danger in time to come, he giveth men occasion, justly and with good conscience, to doubt lest he have not the grace of the Holy Ghost within him, because he is tongue tied and doth not speak'.

The Various Forms of Evangelism

Of course evangelism can take different forms. Ever since Jesus offered living water to the Samaritan woman at Jacob's well

(John 4), and Philip sat beside the Ethiopian in his chariot and told him the good news of Jesus (Acts 8:26ff), *personal evangelism* has had impeccable biblical precedents. It is still vitally important today. While seeking to avoid every taint of aggressive arrogance, it is still our duty, when the opportunity is given and in a spirit of humility, to share Christ with those of our relatives, friends, neighbours and colleagues who do not yet know him.

Mass evangelism too (the preaching of an evangelist to crowds) has over the centuries been signally blessed by God. The recent disgracing of a few American televangelists does not contradict this fact. Besides, Jesus himself proclaimed the good news of the Kingdom to the crowds in Galilee. So did the apostle Paul to the pagans of Lystra (Acts 14) and the philosophers of Athens (Acts 17), and Wesley and Whitefield in eighteenth century Britain and North America. Gifted evangelists of many nationalities are still preaching effectively to large crowds today, although they know that their ministry depends on the active cooperation of churches and Christians. And all over the world there are clergy and lay readers who take their preaching seriously, and who remember that in their congregation there will often be both non-Christians and nominal Christians who need to hear the gospel.

Nevertheless, *local church evangelism* can claim to be the most normal, natural and productive method of spreading the gospel today. There are two main reasons for commending it.

First, there is *the argument from Scripture*. According to the apostle Peter (1 Pet.2:5,9), the Church is both 'a royal priesthood' to offer spiritual sacrifices to God (which is worship) and 'a holy nation' to spread abroad God's praises (which is witness). Moreover, these responsibilities of the universal Church devolve on each local church. Every Christian congregation is called by God to be a worshipping, witnessing community. Indeed, each of these two duties necessarily involves the other. If we truly worship God, acknowledging and adoring his infinite worth, we find ourselves impelled to make him known to others, in order that they may worship him too. Thus worship leads to witness, and witness to worship, in a perpetual circle.

The Thessalonians set a fine example of local church evangelism. Near the beginning of his first letter to them Paul points our this remarkable sequence: 'Our gospel came to you. . . You welcomed the message. . ... The Lord's message rang out from you' (1 Thess.1:5,6,8). In this way the local church becomes like a sounding board which reflects and amplifies the vibrations it receives, or like a radio station which first accepts and then transmits a message. Every church which has heard the gospel must pass it on. This is still God's principal method of evangelism. If all churches had been faithful, the world would long ago have been evangelized.

Secondly, there is *the argument from strategy*. Each local church is situated in a particular neighbourhood. Its first mission responsibility must therefore be to the people who live there. The congregation is strategically placed to reach the parish. Any political party would be wildly jealous of the plant and personnel which are at our disposal. The churches in many countries have ample resources to disseminate the Gospel throughout their land.

Thus biblical theology and practical strategy combine to make the local church the primary agent of evangelism.

But if the local church is to fulfil its God-appointed role, it must first fulfil four conditions. it must (1) *understand* itself (the theology of the Church), (2) *organize* itself (the structures of the Church), (3) *express* itself (the message of the Church), and (4) *be* itself (the life of the Church).

THE CHURCH MUST UNDERSTAND ITSELF
(*OR* THE THEOLOGY OF THE CHURCH)

I make no apology for beginning here. Many churches are sick because they have a false self-image. They have grasped neither who they are (their identity) nor what they are called to be (their vocation). We all know the importance for mental health of having an accurate self-image. What is true of persons is equally true of churches.

At least two false images of the Church are prevalent today.

The Religous Club (*or* Introverted Christianity)

According to this view, the local church somewhat resembles the local golf club, except that the common interest of its members happens to be God rather than golf. They see themselves as religious people who enjoy doing religious things together. They pay their subscription and reckon that they are entitled to certain privileges. In fact, they concentrate on the status and advantages of being club members. They have evidently forgotten – or never known – the perceptive dictum of Archbishop William Temple that 'the Church is the only co-operative society in the world which exists for the benefit of its non-members'. Instead, they are completely introverted, like an ingrown toe- nail. To be sure, Temple was guilty of a slight exaggeration, for church members do have a responsibility to each other, as the many 'one another' verses of the New Testament indicate ('love one another', 'encourage one another', 'bear one another's burdens' etc.). Nevertheless, our primary responsibilities are our worship of God and our mission in the world.

Similar to the club is the circle. We now picture the Church as a group of people who are sitting in a circle and enjoying each other's company. Again, much in this model is good. God means his people to love, serve, support and care for one another. What is wrong with this image, however, is that in facing one another we have turned our backs on the world.

At the opposite extreme to the religious club is:

The Secular Mission (*or* Religionless Christianity)

Many of us remember the 1960s in which some Christian thinkers became understandably exasperated by what they saw as the ecclesiastical self-centredness of the Church. The Church seemed to them so incorrigibly absorbed in its own petty domestic affairs, that they resolved to abandon it and drop it. For the arena of divine service they would exchange the Church for the secular city. They were no longer interested in 'worship services', they said, but only in 'worship service'. So they tried to develop a 'religionless Chrsitianity' in which they re-interpreted worship as mission, love for God as love for neighbour, and prayer to God as encounter with people.

How, nearly thirty years later, should we evaluate this movement? We must surely agree that their distaste for selfish religion was right. Since it is nauseating to God, it ought to sicken us also. But the concept of a 'religionless Christianity' was an unbalanced over-reaction. We have no liberty to confuse worship and mission, even though (as we have seen) each involves the other. There is always an element of mission in worship and of worship in mission, but they are not synonymous.

There is a third way to understand the Church, which combines what is true in both false images, and which recognizes that we have responsibility both to worship God and to serve the world.

The Double Identity of the Church (*or* Incarnational Christianity)

By its 'double identity' we mean that the Church is a people who have been both called out of the world to worship God and sent back into the world to witness and serve. These are, in fact, two of the classical 'marks' of the Church. According to the first, the Church is 'holy', called out to belong to God and to worship him. According to the second, the Church is 'apostolic', sent out into the world on its mission. Alternatively we may say that the Church is summoned by God to be simultaneously 'holy' (distinct from the world) and 'worldly' (not in the sense of assimilating the world's values and standards, but in the sense of renouncing otherworldliness and becoming instead immersed in the life of the world). It was Dr Alec Vidler who, in his book *Essays in Liberality* (1957), admirably captured the Church's double identity by referring to its 'holy worldliness'.

Nobody has ever exhibited the meaning of 'holy worldliness' better than our Lord Jesus Christ. His incarnation is the perfect embodiment of it. He entered our world. He made himself one with us in our frailty. He became vulnerable to our temptations and our pain. He lived our life, experienced our sorrows, bore our sins and died our death. He could not have identified himself with us more completely than he did. Yet in becoming one of us, he did not cease to be himself, for in becoming human he did not cease to be divine. It was total identification without any loss of identity, in other words 'holy worldliness'.

Our mission, then, is to be modelled on his. 'As you sent me into the world', he prayed to his Father, 'I have sent them into the world' (John 17:18; cf. 20:21). We have to enter into other people's worlds, as he entered into ours, into their thought-world (as we struggle to understand their misunderstandings of the gospel), and into their heart-world (as we try to feel their alienation and pain). It is here that the indispensable relation between evangelism and social action becomes plain. In seeking to reach people for Christ, we cannot possibly ignore their social reality, whether it be poverty, homelessness, unemployment or discrimination. We do not enter into another person's world if we close our eyes and our hearts to a large part of it. Archbishop Michael Ramsey put it well in his *Images Old and New* (1967), his critique of secular theology: 'we state and commend the faith only in so far as we get out and put ourselves with loving sympathy inside the doubts of the doubter, the questions of the questioner, and the loneliness of those who have lost the way'. That is the meaning of 'incarnational evangelism'.

Seldom in its long history has the Church managed to preserve its God-given double identity of holy worldliness. Instead, it has tended to oscillate between the two extremes. Sometimes (in an over-emphasis on its holiness) the Church has withdrawn from the world and so has neglected its mission. At other times (in an over-emphasis on its worldliness) it has conformed to the world, assimilating its views and values, and so has neglected its holiness. But in order to fulfil its mission, the Church must faithfully respond to both its calling and preserve both parts of its identity.

'Mission' arises, then, from the biblical doctrine of the Church in the world. If we are not 'the Church', the holy and distinct people of God, we have nothing to say because we are compromised. If, on the other hand, we are not 'in the world', immersed in its life and suffering, we have no one to serve because we are insulated. Our calling is to be 'holy' and 'worldly' at the same time. Without this balanced biblical ecclesiology we will never recover or fulfil our mission.

THE CHURCH MUST ORGANIZE ITSELF (*OR* THE STRUCTURES OF THE CHURCH)

The Church must organize itself in such a way as to express its understanding of itself. Its structures must reflect its theology, especially its double identity.

The commonest fault is for the Church to be structured for 'holiness' rather than 'worldliness', for worship and fellowship rather than mission. This was the emphasis of the report *The Church for Others* (1968), sub-titled 'a quest for structures for missionary congregations'. One does not have to agree with everything in the book in order to appreciate its thrust that 'the missionary Church is not concerned with itself – it is a church for others. . . Its centre lies outside itself; it must live "ex-centredly". . . The church has to turn itself outwards to the world. . . We have to recognize that the churches have developed into "waiting churches" into which people are expected to come. Its inherited structures stress and embody this static outlook. One may say that we are in danger of perpetuating "come-structures" instead of replacing them by "go-structures". One may say that inertia has replaced the dynamism of the gospel and of participation in the mission of God'. Further, our static, inflexible, self-centred structures are 'heretical structures' because they embody a heretical doctrine of the Church.

Some zealous churches organize an overfull programme of church-based activities. Something is arranged for every night of the week. On Monday night the committees meet, and on Tuesday night the fellowship groups. On Wednesday night the Bible study takes place, and on Thursday night the prayer meeting. Even on Friday and Saturday evenings other good causes occupy people's time and energy. Such churches give the impression that their main goal is to keep their members out of mischief! Certainly they have neither time nor opportunity to get into mischief since they are busily engaged in the church every single night of the week!

But such a crowded, church-centred programme, admirable as it may look at first sight, has many drawbacks and dangers. To begin with, it is detrimental to Christian family life. Marriages break up and families distinegrate because father and /or mother are seldom at home. It also inhibits church members from getting involved in the local community because they are preoccupied with the local church. It thus contradicts an essential part of the Church's identity, namely its 'worldliness'. As Bishop Richard Wilke of the United Methodist Church in the United States put it in his book *And Are We Yet Alive?* (1986), 'our structure has become an end in itself, not a means of saving the world'. In that case it is a heretical structure.

I sometimes wonder (although I exaggerate in order to make my point) if it would not be very healthy for church members to

meet only on Sundays (for worship, fellowship and teaching) and
not at all midweek. Then we would gather on Sundays and
scatter for the rest of the week. We would come to Christ for
worship and go for Christ in mission. And in that rhythm of
Sunday-weekday, gathering-scattering, coming-going and
worship-mission the Church would express its holy worldliness,
and its structure would conform to its double identity.

How, then, should the local church organize itself? Ideally, it
seems to me, every five or ten years each church should conduct
a survey in order to evaluate itself and especially to discover how
far its structures reflect its identity. In fact, it should conduct
two surveys, one of the local community and the other of the
local church, in order to learn how far the Church is penetrating
the community for Christ. This idea was recently taken up in
Britain by ACUPA (the Archbishop's Commission on Urban
Priority Areas), whose influential report was entitled *Faith in the
City* (1986). It recommended what is called a 'local church audit',
consisting of both 'the church profile' ('to build up an accurate
picture of the local church') and 'the parish profile' ('to build up
an accurate picture of the parish'). Perhaps I could take these in
the opposite order:

A Local Community Survey

Each church is set in a particular situation, and needs to become
familiar with it in all its particularity. A questionnaire will need
to be drawn up. Here are some of the questions which it will
probably include:

1. What sort of people live in our parish? What is their ethnic
origin, nationality, religion, culture, media preference, and
work? Are these normal families, single-parent families, single
people, senior citizens, young people? What are the parish's
main social needs, relating to housing, employment, poverty,
education?

2. Has the parish any centres of education, whether schools,
colleges, adult education centres, or play groups?

3. What places of business are found in it? Factories, farms,
offices, shops, or studios? Is there significant unemployment?

4. Where do the people live? Do they occupy houses or flats,
and do they own or rent them? Are there any hotels, hostels,

student residences, apartment blocks, or homes for senior citizens?

5. Where do people congregate when they are at leisure? Cafe or restaurant, pub or disco, shopping mall, youth club or other clubs, bingo hall, concert hall, dance hall, theatre or cinema, sports ground or park?

6. What public services have their headquarters locally? Police, fire brigade, prison, hospital, public library, other social services?

7. Are there other religious buildings – church or chapel, synagogue, mosque, temple, or Christian Science reading room?

8. Has the community changed in the last ten years, and what changes can be forecast during the next ten?

In each case the group charged with making this survey will be expected to ask two further questions: What contact has the church with this variegated community? And what impact is it making? If the survey is conducted with thoroughness, the church will probably receive a shock. It will be surprised, even mortified, to discover that whole segments of the parish are untouched by the gospel and are totally secularized.

A Local Church Survey

In this second survey probing questions will need to be asked. Is the Church in reality organized only for itself, for its own survival and convenience, and for the preservation of its privileges? Is it organized to serve itself, or to serve God and the community? What are its cherished traditions and conventions which unnecessarily separate it from the community? The questionnaire might include the following areas:

The Church Building
Church members tend to be most interested in its *interior* (its beauty, comfort and amenities). But we also need to walk round it and look at it through the eyes of an *outsider*. What image does it present? Is it a fortress (dark, forbidding and austere), or is it bright, inviting and welcoming? As an illustration, let me mention visiting the huge central square of the capital city of a Latin American Republic. In the middle was the statue of the national hero, who had rescued the country at the beginning of

the last century from the Spanish *conquistadores*. One side of the
square was entirely occupied by the Roman Catholic cathedral. I
tried to get in, but it was closed. On the steps leading up to its
main door, however, were three human beings – a drunk who
had vomited copiously, a blind beggar selling matches, and a
prostitute who was offering herself to passers-by in broad
daylight. A drunk, a beggar and a prostitute, three symbols of
human tragedy, and behind them a locked cathedral, which
seemed to be saying 'Keep out! We don't want you.' I realize that
there may have been good reasons why the cathedral was closed.
My concern is with the 'vibes' which were given off by that
scene.

A critical look at the inside of the church building will be
necessary too, espcially through the eyes of non-Christian visitors
– its decoration and furniture, lighting and heating, its
noticeboards, posters, bookstall and leaflets.

The Church Services.

As with the first century Jewish synagogue, so with the twentieth
century Christian Church, there are 'godfearers' on the edge of
every congregation, who are attracted but not yet committed to
Christ. Are our services exclusively for the committed, designed
only for the initiated, and therefore mumbo-jumbo to outsiders?
Or do we remember the fringe members and non-members who
may be present? What about the forms of service, the liturgy and
language, the music (words, tunes and instruments), the seating,
and the dress of both clergy and congregation? We need to ask
ourselves what vibrations all these things give out.

The Church Membership

Is our membership mobilized for mission? Or is our church so
clericalized (i.e. clergy-dominated) as to make this impossible?
Has it grasped the New Testament teaching about the 'every
member ministry of the Body of Christ'? Or is it less a body than
a pyramid, with the clergy at the pinnacle and the lay people in
their serried ranks of inferiority at the base? Are the members of
the church also members of the community? Or are they either
confined to church activities or practising a commuter-
Christianity (travelling long distances to church), which makes
local involvement difficult, even artificial?

The Church Programme.

Do we imprison our members in the church? Or do we deliberately release at least some of them (including leaders) from church commitments in order to encourage them to be active for Christ in the community, and then support them with our interest and prayers as they do so? Do we ensure that the biblical truth of the double identity of the Church is taught and embodied, and that training is available for those who want to commit themselves to Christian service and witness?

The two surveys (of community and church) will need to be studied by the Church Council both separately and in relation to each other. Out of this reflection will grow a strategy for mission. The Council (preferably with others who may wish to be involved) will set both long-term and short-term goals, and establish a list of priorities. They may decide that the church is suffering from a false self-image and needs above all else some biblical teaching on its holy worldliness and on the implications of this for mission; or that a training programme must be arranged to equip members for evangelism; or that church-based activities should be reduced in order to increase members' involvement in the community. It might be decided to restructure radically the church building, decor, seating or services; or to organize a general visitation of the parish, if possible in co-operation with other local churches; or to form specialist groups to penetrate particular, secular segments of the parish. For example, a group of committed young people could adopt a local disco, not in order to make occasional evangelistic raids into it, but between them (in pairs) to visit it regularly over a long period, in order to make friends with the other young people who congregate there. Again, the church may decide to arrange home meetings for neighbours, or a series of apologetic lectures in a local and neutral building, or regular guest services with an evangelistic thrust, to which members would be encouraged to bring their friends. Or the church may determine to take up some special social need in the parish which has surfaced during the surveys, and encourage a group to study it and then recommend action. All such decision will be designed to help the church to identify with the community and develop an authentically incarnational mission.

THE CHURCH MUST EXPRESS ITSELF
(*OR* THE MESSAGE OF THE CHURCH)

It is not enough for the local church to understand itself and organize itself accordingly; it must also articulate its message. For evangelism, at its simplest and most basic, is sharing the evangel. So in order to define evangelism we must also define the good news.

There can be no doubt that the essence of the Gospel is Jesus Christ himself. It would be impossible to preach the Christian good news without talking about Jesus. So we read that Philip, speaking to the Ethiopian, 'told him the good news about Jesus' (Acts 8:35), and that the apostle Paul described himself as 'set apart for the Gospel of God. . . regarding his Son. . .' (Rom.1:1,3). Moreover, in bearing witness to Jesus we must speak above all of his death and resurrection. To quote Paul again in his famous summary of the apostolic Gospel, 'what I received I passed on to you as of first importance: that Christ died for our sins according to the Scriptures, that he was buried, that he was raised on the third day according to the Scriptures, and that he appeared. . .' (1 Corinthians 15:3,4). We simply do not share the Gospel if we do not declare God's love in the gift of his Son to live our life, to die for our sins and to rise again, together with his offer through Jesus Christ, to all who repent and believe, of a new life of forgiveness and freedom, and of membership in his new society. The primates' recommended definition includes these essentials.

But how shall we formulate this good news in our world's increasingly pluralistic societies, in such a way that it resonates with them and makes sense? There are two opposite extremes to avoid.

The first extreme I will call *total fixity*. Some Christian people seem to be in bondage to words and formulae, and so become prisoners of a gospel stereotype. They wrap up their message in a nice, neat package; and they tape, label and price-tag it as if it were destined for the supermarket. Then, unless their favourite phraseology is used (whether the Kingdom of God or the blood of Jesus or human liberation or being born again or justification by faith or the cosmic lordship of Christ), they roundly declare that the Gospel has not been preached. What these people seem not to have noticed is the rich diversity of gospel formulation which is found in the New Testament itself. The options I have listed are all biblical, but because all of them contain an element of imagery, and each image is different, it is impossible to fuse them into a single, simple concept. So it is perfectly legitimate to develop one or other of them, according to what seems most appropriate to the occasion.

The opposite extreme is *total fluidity*. Some years ago I heard a British bishop say: 'there's no such thing as the Gospel in a vacuum. You don't even know what the Gospel is until you enter each particular situation. You have to enter the situation first, and then you discover the Gospel when you're there.' Now if he meant that he wanted a gospel in context not in vacuum, and that we need to relate the Gospel sensitively to each person and situation, I am in full agreement with him: but to say 'there is no such thing as the gospel in a vacuum' and 'you discover it' in each situation is surely a serious overstatement. For what the advocates of total fluidity seem not to have noticed is that, alongside the New Testament's rich diversity of gospel formulation, there is also an underlying unity (especially regarding the saving death and resurrection of Jesus) which brings the different formulations together. As Professor A.M. Hunter wrote in his *The Unity of the New Testament* (1943), 'there is . . . a deep unity in the New Testament, which dominates and transcends all the diversities.'

Is there a middle way? Yes, there is. Both the extremes which I have described express important concerns which need to be preserved. the first ('total fixity') rightly emphasizes that the gospel has been revealed by God and received by us. It is both a *paradosis* (a tradition to be preserved) and a *parathēkē* (a deposit to be guarded). We did not invent it, and we have no liberty to edit it or tamper with it. The second ('total fluidity') rightly emphasizes that the Gospel must be contextualized, that is to say, related appropriately to each particular person or situation. Otherwise it will be perceived as irrelevant.

Somehow, then, we have to learn to combine these two proper concerns. We have to wrestle with the dialectic between the ancient Word and the modern world, between that has been given and what has been left open, between content and context, Scripture and culture, revelation and contextualization. We need more fidelity to Scripture and more sensitivity to people. Not one without the other, but both.

THE CHURCH MUST BE ITSELF
(*OR* THE LIFE OF THE CHURCH)

The Church is supposed to be God's new society, the living embodiment of the Gospel, a sign of the Kingdom of God, a demonstration of what human community looks like when it comes under his gracious rule.

In other words, God's purpose is that the good news of Jesus Christ is set forth visually as well as verbally, or in the language of the primates' definition, that it be made known 'by word and deed'. Every educator knows how much easier it is for human beings to learn through what they see and experience than through what they hear. Or rather, word and deed, hearing and seeing belong essentially together. This is certainly so in evangelism. People have to see with their own eyes that the gospel we preach has transformed us. As John Poulton put it in his book *A Today Sort of Evangelism* (1972), 'Christians. . . need to look like what they are talking about. It is *people* who communicate primarily, not words or ideas. . . What communicates now is basically personal authenticity'. Conversely, if our life contradicts our message, our evangelism will lack all credibility. Indeed, the greatest hindrance to evangelism is lack of integrity in the evangelist.

No text has helped me to understand the implications of this for the life of the local church more than 1 John 4:12 'No-one has ever seen God, but if we love one another, God lives in us and his love is made complete in us'. God is invisible. Nobody has ever seen him. All that human beings have ever seen of him is glimpses of his glory, of the outshining of his being.

Now the invisibility of God is a great problem for faith. It was for the Jews in the Old Testament. Their heathen neighbours laughed at them for actually worshipping an invisible God. 'You say you believe in God?' they taunted them. 'Where is he? Come to our temples and we will show you are gods. They have ears and eyes, hands and feet, and mouths and noses too. But where is you God? We can't see him. Ha, ha, ha!' The Jews found this ridicule hard to bear. Hence the complaint of psalmist and prophet 'why do the nations say "where is their God?" ' (e.g. Psalm 115:2). Of course Israel had its own apologetic. The idols of the heathen were nothing, only the work of human hands. True, they had mouths, but they could not speak, ears but could not hear, noses but could not smell, hands but could not feel, and feet but could not walk (e.g Psalm 115:4–7). Yahweh, on the other hand, although (being spirit) he had no mouth, had spoken; although he had no ears, he listened to Israel's prayers; and although he had not hands, he had both created the universe and redeemed his people by his mighty power. At the same time, the people of God longed that he would make himself known to the nations, so that they might see him and believe in him.

The same problem of an unseen God challenges us today, espcially young people who have been brought up on the scientific method. They are taught to examine everything by their five senses. Anything which is not amenable to empirical investigation they are told to suspect and even reject. So could it ever be reasonable to believe in an invisible God? 'Let us only see him', they say, 'and we will believe.'

How then has God solved the problem of his own invisibility? First and foremost he has done so by sending his Son into the world. 'No-one has ever seen God: the only Son, who is in the bosom of the Father, he has made him known.' (John 1:18 RSV). Consequently Jesus could say 'anyone who has seen me has seen the Father' (John 14:9), and Paul could describe him as 'the (visible) image of the invisible God' (Colossians 1:15).

To this people tend to reply: 'That is truly wonderful, but it happened nearly 2,000 years ago. Is there no way in which the invisible God makes himself visible *today?*' Yes, there is. 'No-one has ever seen God' (1 John 4:12). John begins this verse in his first letter with the identical sentence which he has used in the prologue in his gospel (John 1:18). But now he concludes the sentence differently. In the Gospel he wrote that 'the only Son . . . has made him known'. In the Epistle he writes that 'if we love one another, God lives in us and his love is made complete in us'. Because of John's deliberate repetition of the same statement, this can only mean one thing. The invisible God, who once made himself visible in Christ, now makes himself visible in Christians, *if we love one another*.

God is love in his essential being, and has revealed his love in the gift of his Son to live and die for us. Now he calls us to be a community of love, loving each other in the intimacy of his family – especially across the barriers of age and sex, race and rank – and loving the world he loves in its alienation, hunger, poverty and pain. It is through the quality of our loving that God makes himself visible today.

We cannot proclaim the Gospel of God's love with any degree of integrity if we do not exhibit it in our love for others. Perhaps nothing is so damaging to the cause of Christ as a church which is either torn apart by jealousy, rivalry, slander and malice, or preoccupied with its own selfish concerns. Such churches urgently need to be radically renewed in love. As one of the group reports of the 1978 Lambeth Conference put it, 'mission without renewal is hypocrisy'. It is only if we love one another that the world will believe that Jesus is the Christ and that we are his disciples (John 13:35; 17:21).

Here, then, are the four main prerequistes for evangelism through the local church. First the church must understand itself (theologically), grasping its double identity. Secondly it must organize itself (structurally), developing a mission strategy which reflects its double identity. Thirdly, it must express itself (verbally), articulating its gospel in a way which is both faithful to Scripture and relevant to the contemporary world. And fourthly, it must be itself (morally and spiritually), becoming so completely transformed into a community of love that through it the invisible God again makes himself visible to the world.

Footnotes

Possible questions for group discussion

1. 'A dumb Christian'. What do you think are the main reasons why we Anglicans are often tongue-tied?
2. Try to develop your own arguments for the importance of evangelism through the local church.
3. Reflect together on incarnation and ministry of Jesus Christ as a model for Christian mission today.
4. What changes would your church need to make if it were to express its 'holy worldliness' better?
5. Take one of the two suggested questionnaires, and consider how it would need to be adapted and/or amplified in order to suit your church or parish.
6. Begin to develop the kind of evangelistic strategy which you would like to recommend your church to adopt.
7. Granted a necessary flexibility in our presentation of the Gospel, how would you express its essentials which are always and everywhere true? You may like to take the primates' suggested definition of evangelism as your basis.
8. What are the features of your church's life which put people off and hinder the Gospel? What practical steps could be taken to change these things?

Chapter Three

Evangelism with Theological Credibility

David Evans

"The Gospel is true always and everywhere, or it is not a Gospel at all, or true at all". *William Temple*.

Introduction

Lord Jenkins of Hillshead, former U.K. Home Secretary and now Chancellor of Oxford University, was recently invited to give a "Keynote paper" on the pros and cons of tourism in the U.K. He wrote:

"Last week I delivered the 'keynote address' at an international conference on tourism and conservation in Canterbury. The dictionary definition of 'keynote' is 'a central or determining principle in a speech, literary work etc'. In practice it means that you have no particular expertise to impart and are therefore allowed to amble around the perimeter of the conference subject in any order that strikes you as convenient."[1]

I propose therefore to amble around the perimeter . . . but I trust in a helpful panoramic style.

1 Evangelism and Authority
2 Evangelism and Definitions
3 Evangelism and Mission
4 Evangelism and Culture
5 Evangelism and Christ
6 Evangelism and Challenge Today

Evangelism and Authority

In North America recently I came across the understanding of Anglican Authority as being like a three legged stool of

David Evans

Scripture, Tradition and Reason. In the U.K. the Osborne report on homosexuality spoke openly of the three sources of Anglican Authority. These expressions may not yet be universally accepted but they are frequently implied by the threefold reference to Scripture, Tradition and Reason. We are straying far from our historical origins. Even Trent and Vatican II only spoke of two sources not three, and Vatican II repudiated the two source theory, returning in principle to the ancient and normative single source of Scripture. Our Anglican formularies clearly refer to one normative source. They do not speak of scripture as *a* normative source (à la ARCIC) or of two or even three sources. I believe we are bowing to a widespread "folk religion" approach. I believe we are adopting a sophisticated unwillingness to take sides in controversial debates and in the end pretend to a false intellectual humility. Jesus was more prepared to *be* a "sign of contradiction" that people spoke against, because He had adopted an authoritative position (re adultery for instance) than to be ready to live with contradictions, sitting on the fence.

It has of course been clearly pointed out that reason anyway cannot constitute a source of authority. It is merely the rational process by which we assess the at times conflicting claims of Scripture and Tradition, and of course tradition historically refers to Apostolic Tradition or that of the Early Church Fathers and Councils in so far as it agrees with or spells out the teaching of Scripture. Tradition is not another name for 20th Century experience or the latest theory of a university professor or theologian, whose views tie in with a more up to date laissez-faire moral stance or a supposedly more intellectually acceptable scientific explanation of Christian doctrine (e.g. in the homosexuality debate). Tradition is not equal to or more important than Scripture. We are not free subjectively to choose whichever suits us. Of course it is Anglican to seek to achieve a balance of Scripture, Tradition and Reason. We are not so blind as to pretend that tradition plays no part in the life of our church. Nor are we so obscurantist as to claim that our rational powers do not influence us in assessing truth. We claim no infallibility in our interpretative processes. But if councils have erred, so can and do lesser bodies and even more so individuals.

Scripture, Tradition and Reason do not form a three legged stool on which the Anglican Communion is perched. Nor do we have three sources of authority. We need to return more to the position defined thus:

We have *reverence* for Scripture, as the normative source of authority;

We have *respect* for Tradition as the historical out working of revealed truth in different cultural settings;

We have *recourse* to Reason as the God given faculty for receiving scriptural truth and sifting tradition as God's Spirit enlightens our minds.

I want to add two short postscripts to this section on Evangelism and Authority.

First the widespread rejection of the many prevalent fundamentalisms of our era leads to an attitude undermining of the written word. It is not thought acceptable to take seriously any actual biblical "proof text", because it is assumed that we shall be taking it out of its context and therefore distorting it. Rather we are encouraged to embrace a general view of what the Christian tradition teaches, which often proves a highly subjective evaluation. Two examples will illustrate my meaning. The assertion that the Bible is world-affirming rather than world-denying overlooks the diversity of, for instance, John's use of the word "world". The assertion that our doctrine of the Church must be inclusivist disregards much material that is exclusive.

Second, a further, no doubt unintentional, downgrading of Scripture is observable in some of those parts of the church affected by the Charismatic movement. There is less exposition of Scripture, more experience sharing, much emphasis on contemporary prophecy and much interest in visions and pictures etc. These result in a distancing from the biblical text and an increasing unfamiliarity with the whole counsel of God through lack of regular exposure to it.

Evangelism and Definitions

At Lausanne I in 1974 John Stott referred to the celebrated

conversation between Alice in Wonderland and Humpty Dumpty:

> "When *I* use a word" Humpty Dumpty said in a rather scornful tone, "it means just what I choose it to mean. Neither more nor less."

> "The question is", said Alice, "whether you *can* make words mean different things". "The question is", said Humpty Dumpty, "which is to be master – that's all."

> The issue between Alice and Humpty Dumpty – whether man can manipulate the meaning of words or whether words have an autonomy which cannot be infringed – is still a contemporary issue. The modern church sometimes seems like a kind of theological wonderland in which numerous Humpty Dumptys enjoy playing with words and making them mean what they want them to mean.

Are we basically to seek a definition of evangelism from the Bible or are we at liberty to "take our agenda from the present world-scene"? There is a tension between faithfulness to revelation and the temptation to be relevant.

Back in 1975 in *Evangelii Nuntiandi* (Evangelization in the Modern World) we read in paragraph 18:-

> 18. For the Church, evangelizing means bringing the Good News into all the strata of humanity, and through its influence transforming humanity from within and making it new: "Now I am making the whole of creation new". But there is no new humanity if there are not first of all new persons renewed by Baptism and by lives lived according to the Gospel. The purpose of evangelization is therefore precisely this interior change, and if it had to be expressed in one sentence the best way of stating it would be to say that the Church evangelizes when she seeks to convert, solely through the divine power of the Message she proclaims, both the personal and collective consciences of people, the activities in which they engage, and the lives and concrete milieux which are theirs.

In April 1989 the Anglican Primates from Larnace, Cyprus wrote:- "To evangelise is to make known by word and deed the love of the crucified and risen Christ in the power of the Holy Spirit, so that people will repent, believe and receive Christ as their Saviour and obediently serve Him as their Lord in the fellowship of His Church".

In 1987 the Stuttgart consultation on evangelism quoted with approval the statement in *Mission and Evangelism: An Ecumenical Affirmation* (WCC) "The proclamation of the Gospel includes an invitation to recognize and accept in a personal decision the saving lordship of Christ. It is the announcement of a personal encounter mediated by the Holy Spirit, with the living Christ, receiving his forgiveness and making a personal acceptance of the call for discipleship and a new life of service".[2]

Endless definitions of evangelism have been made, some like Pope Paul VI's above merge into a definition of mission. Three points would seem to be clear:-

Evangelism must not be defined in terms of its results.
The biblical usage of evangelism is the announcement of good news, irrespective of results. We may take exception therefore to the Anglican Primates' definition which has its roots in the 1919 Archbishop's "Committee of Enquiry into the Evangelistic work of the church". And I refer to the word "so".

Evangelism must not be defined in terms of methods.
Philip was both a mass evangelist in Samaria and a personal evangelist to the Ethiopian. Nor must evangelism be rejected out of hand because of disagreement with any particular method used by a particular person or group of people.

Evangelism must in fact be defined in terms of the message.
In his commentary on Acts, John Stott refers to the gospel events, the gospel witnesses (apostolic interpreters) and the gospel promises and the gospel demands. This confronts the modern listener with the scandal of historical particularity. Unless there is acceptance of Gospel parameters we can end up with some such statement as "everything the Church is and does is evangelism". No wonder that the question can then be: "In our day, what has happened to that hidden energy of the Good News, which is able to have a powerful effect on man's conscience and that evangelical force which is capable of really transforming the people of this century?"[3]

Evangelism and Mission

In recent years a large amount of time has been expended on seeking to relate the various components of holistic mission.

Some see mission and evangelism as synonymous and yet can interpret evangelism as everything from the "winning of souls for eternity as the church's unique task" to a "this worldly programme of the humanization of society".

Others distinguish between evangelism and mission in different ways or refer to evangelism and evangelization or drop mission altogether because of its colonial vibrations and broaden evangelism to embrace "human development, liberation, justice and peace and the integrity of creation".

A suggested clarification of terminology might look like this – *Mission* is the umbrella term for the church's God given task in the world which comprises –

Continuous *evangelism* of men, women and children of every race.
Compassionate *service* of those in need.
Integral *transformation* of society.

These components are complementary and not interchangeable. They should be intertwined in an organic and balanced outreach. Practically their relative priority is affected by different cultural and socio-political contexts, but basically they are indispensable and equal partners.

I find Luke 4: 18, 19, an important link passage between Old and New Testaments. When interpreted from the point of view of what Jesus actually did in His incarnational ministry, it was his programme pronouncement, and therefore should guide our "own agenda".

"The Spirit of the Lord is upon me, because he has anointed me to preach good news to the poor
(i) to proclaim freedom for the prisoners and recovery of sight for the blind
(ii) to release the oppressed
(iii) to proclaim the year of the Lord's favour."

This is a comprehensive programme not to be forced either into a narrow spiritualised and pietistic message or into a wideranging revolutionary manifesto. The annunciation of Good News in proclaimed word and liberating deed is directed to all who are humble and open enough to receive it, whether enslaved by wealth or diminished by poverty. The basic indispensable requirement for Jesus himself in this task, as for us, in this is the Holy Spirit's anointing. And we can expect no different a response than the furious reaction from those with vested interests nor, indeed, should constant division among his hearers surprise us.

Evangelism and Culture

The proper contextualization of evangelism has also been at the forefront of recent discussion. And it is in this area that we especially hope to make a worthwhile contribution through the Mombasa consultation. I will do little more here than quote from Bishop David Jenkins' 1988 Lambeth presentation on Evangelisation and Culture:

"This means that primary *evangelisation must be local, ecumenical, social and human*. The engagement of evangelisation must be that of the *local* church. Assistance may be brought in from outside but words from strangers can rarely alter people in, at any rate, most modern cultures, to the possibility of God. This requires local, daily and neighbourly living and sharing. Seeing that any evangelisation which is consistent with the New Testament cannot be recruitment to our brand of religion but must be an alerting to the universal kingdom of the true and living God, evangelisation must be *ecumenical*. Churches which compete to recruit are, in practice, destroying the message and the credibility of the gospel. The engagement must be *social* for the wrath of God, which is an active sign and power of the holy love of the kingdom, is in conflict with all that we do in our social structures, political policies and economic exploitations which diminish persons in God's image and abuse the created world which is God's gift. Finally evangelisation must be *human*. The living God fights against all idols in the name and person and resurrection of Jesus in order that those human beings for whom Christ died might be caught up into the glory of his fulfilled creation as their best selves, fulfilled in the particularity of person, race, language and culture, to make their particular contribution to the kingdom and city of God. Therefore evangelisation must cherish the particular humanity, gift, language and culture of each and every one of us. The glory of the gospel is that each and everyone of us by name is invited to repent, to be saved from idols, distortion and death and to be part of God's city, kingdom and eternity."

This emphasis on the local, ecumenical, social and human should not however constitute a sellout to any particular cultural setting. John Stott in his Acts commentary writes:

"When we contrast much contemporary evangelism with Paul's its shallowness is immediately shown up. Our evangelism tends to be too *ecclesiastical* (inviting people to church), whereas Paul also took the gospel out into the secular world; *too emotional* (with appeals to decision without an adequate basis of understanding), whereas Paul taught, reasoned and tried to persuade; and *too superficial* (making brief encounters and expecting quick results), whereas Paul stayed in Corinth and Ephesus for five years, faithfully sowing gospel seed and in due time reaping a harvest."[4]

Evangelism and Christ

Clearly the question of the uniqueness of Christ in an age of "towards a theology for Inter-Faith Dialogue" has become another central issue. *The Gospel in a Pluralistic Society* (Lesslie Newbigin) highlights the present Western concern, though Michael Nazir Ali reminds us that the West is evidencing a lack of historical consciousness as inter-faith encounter has been a fact of life for centuries in non-Western plural situations. And the N.T. and O.T. have much more to contribute than is often accepted. However the current scene is very much dominated by an inclusivist model for the church. There is a shift from the historical Christ to a cosmic Christ and we are told that trinitarian religion gives us more flexibility than a narrow Christology. The biblical statements of "uncompromising exclusivity" are scorned (Jesus 'no other way', Paul's 'no other mediator', Peter's 'no other name' and Hebrews' *epifrax*).

Michael Nazir Ali in his additional chapter in *Towards a theology for Inter-Faith Dialogue* questions seriously the current doctrine of the *Logos spermatikos* as present in other religions and stresses that the Word has *become* flesh, not simply manifested itself in flesh. Jesus Christ is therefore the full, definitive and final revelation of God for us. The same attempt to posit a benign spiritual influence distanced from the Holy Spirit of the Bible is also criticized. The Manila Manifesto from Lausanne II dedicates a whole section to this area and concludes: "We are determined to bear a positive and uncompromising witness to the uniqueness of our Lord in his life, death and resurrection, in all aspects of our evangelistic work including inter-faith dialogue".

More recently the Archbishop of York wrote: "To put it bluntly I am a Christian because I believe Christianity is true and valuable in a sense which other faiths cannot match. I believe there are good arguments for its truths, both intellectual and practical, which are not impaled on the relativist hook to the point where assertions of faith are reduced to mere expressions of opinion".[5]

Evangelism and Challenge Today.

The manifesto at Manila of 1989 outlined clearly the present challenge that the whole Church is called to take the whole gospel to the whole world just as the Lausanne Covenant of 1974 committed its members to pray, to plan and to work together for the evangelisation of the whole world. "Christian evangelism presupposes the good news of Jesus Christ and becomes possible and effective only when the Church recovers both the biblical gospel and a joyful confidence in its truth, relevance and power."[6] The challenge is reiterated in other language in *The Churchman Preface* published to coincide with the appearance of Crockford's Clerical Directory 1989–1990:

"Ours is often called a post-Christian society, and it is certainly true that the acids of modernity have burned away the plausibility of dogmatic Christianity, but have not diminished the hunger for God that is found in the human heart".[7]

"The call to evangelism must be a call to recover the central glory of Anglicanism, because the alternatives are bleak. On the one hand there is the arrogance, over-confidence and cruelty of the fundamentalist religions of all brands, which cater to the worst aspects of our human insecurity. On the other hand there are those who would draw us away from the knowledge of the true God altogether into a kind of solipsistic despair. An honest evangelism must steer a precarious and exhilarating course between these two imposters, between the rocks and the desert, between the arrogance of overbelief and the cynicism of unbelief."[8]

Then indeed we shall be responding aright to the challenge of evangelism with theological credibility.

Footnotes

1. *The Independent* Weekend Review, April 7, 1990.
2. The Statement of the Stuttgart Consultation on Evangelism 1987 in *Proclaiming Christ in Christ's Way: Studies in Integral Evangelism* edited by Vinay Samuel and Albrecht Hauser (Oxford, Regnum, 1989).
3. *Evangelii Nuntiandi* 4.
4. John R.W. Stott *The Message of Acts* (Leicester, Inter-Varsity Press, 1989) p 314.
5. In *The Independent* Newspaper, June 3 1989.
6. John Stott, *The Message of Acts* op. cit., p 144.
7. *The Churchman Preface* (Churchman Publishing, 1989) p 83.
8. *The Churchman Preface* op. cit., p 84.

Bibliography

1. Towards the Conversion of England: A plan dedicated to the memory of Archbishop William Temple Lausanne I 1975.
2. Let the Earth Hear His Voice: Lausanne I edited by J. Douglas (World-Wide Publications, 1975).
3. Evangelization in the Modern World: Evangelii Nuntiandi Pope Paul VI 1975.
4. Statement of the Stuttgart Consultation on Evangelism 1987 in *Proclaiming Christ in Christs Way Studies in Integral Evangelism*, edited by Vinay Samuel and Albrecht Hause, (Oxford, Regnum 1989).
5. Mission and Evangelization: An Ecumenical Affirmation Emilio Castro (Genwa, W.C.C., 1982).
6. *The Message of Acts:* J.R.W.Stott (IVP, 1990).
7. "Evangelisation and Culture": Bishop David Jenkins Lambeth Conference 1988.
8. *The Gospel in a Pluralistic Society:* Lesslie Newbigin (SPCK, 1989).
9. *The Truth Shall Make You Free: The Lambeth Conference* (ACC, 1988).
10. *Towards a theology for Inter-Faith Dialogue.* (ACC, 1986).
11. The Manila Manifesto: Lausanne II 1989.
12. *The Churchman Preface* (Churchman Publishing, 1989).

Chapter Four

Biblical Reflections

Christopher Wright

We began each day with worship and biblical reflection. We were led in meditation on Ezekiel 18 by Andrew Knowles, on John 4 by Juliet Thomas and on Acts 3–4 by Emmanuel Gbonigi. This chapter is not an exhaustive exposition of these passages, but a digest of the reflections of the speakers and comments of the group in the discussion that followed.

EZEKIEL 18
EVANGELISM IN A CONTEXT OF COMMUNITY COMPLAINT

The chapter starts from a proverb (2). In all societies, and even in atheistic contexts, people use proverbs that assume some personal reality in charge of events. In this case, the exilic community was angry with God and accused him of being unjust. Why should their generation have to suffer for the sins of previous generations of Israel? "The fathers eat sour grapes and the children's teeth are set on edge." Ezekiel's evangelistic purpose is to move the community to repentance and new life (30–32). But before he can do that he has to clear away this complaint and deal with the misunderstanding that underlies it.

Responsibility

Ezekiel meets the proverb head on and simply bans it! Each person bears responsibility for himself before God, in each generation. The person who sins will be the one who suffers death for it. Biblical scholars no longer take the view that Ezekiel was here introducing the idea of individual responsibility for the first time. The whole Old Testament, in the law and the narratives, presupposes and illustrates personal moral responsibility before God. Ezekiel's point was to give fresh emphasis to that truth to a people who were trying to absolve themselves from their own accountability by shifting all the blame to previous generations. So he teaches that God will deal with each generation and individual according to their own moral behaviour, not according to the merits or demerits of their fathers. This, incidentally, does not contradict the balancing truth that the behaviour of one generation does affect future generations. Wickedness bears long term fruit, as the second commandment shows (Ex. 20:5). But that did not mean that one person could be punished for the sin of another (Deut. 24:16).

To make his point, Ezekiel launches into an ethical case study that spans three generations. The threefold repetition of the categories of righteousness and wickedness is like a moral checklist. It opens a window on the Old Testament understanding of typical good and evil. The list of moral items is close to the ten commandments and also overlaps with similar lists such as Samuel's and Job's self-defences (1 Sam: 12 2–5, Job 31). The sins that the righteous man avoids include: idolatry, adultery, oppression by exploiting debt, robbery, taking interest and judicial corruption.

The list is not just negative, however. There are balancing positive actions. The righteous man not only does not oppress, he returns pledges. He not only does not steal, he feeds the hungry and clothes the naked. He not only exercises self-control when there is an opportunity for wrong-doing, but is actively impartial in judgement. There are definite echoes of Jesus' moral teaching here, in that failure to do positive good is as much a sin as doing actual wrong.

The effect of the three generational model is to show that although good and evil have long term effects, this is no excuse for individuals failing to face up to their own responsibility before God. That is a challenge in the present. Israel tended to look either to the past (e.g. the exodus and historical traditions) or to the future (the prophetic, messianic hope). God wanted them to face the present. There is a "now" about responding to God. We too are good at analysing the past and forecasting the future but God looks for a response now. This highlights the definite need for evangelism among the children of those who are already Christians. Each generation must actively turn to God and choose righteousness.

Evangelism

The evangelistic appeal of Ezekiel's message also opens a window on God's heart. God longs for each individual to turn and live, because every living person belongs to him (4, 30). The chapter expresses the dignity and value of every human being. God takes no pleasure in destructive judgement. Since it is God's desire for each individual not to die, it is therefore our responsibility to take the Gospel to each. The same theology of God's universal love and saving desire underlies Paul's instruction that the church should engage in every kind of prayer for every kind of people (1 Tim. 2:1–7).

It is significant that though the chapter has an evangelistic purpose, as is clear in the appeal at the end, it has a strongly ethical thrust as well. Ezekiel is not preaching six foot above reality, but talks about real human life in terms that his hearers would recognize, ramming home his message with sheer repetition. Righteousness is given practical content. So is repentance, in terms reminiscent of John the Baptist. The stress on ethical discernment and moral effort contradicts the popular idea that true spiritual life is just to "let go and let Jesus". "Rid yourselves . . ." (31) calls for deliberate moral choice and action, similar to Peter's exhortation in 1 Peter 2:1.

On the other hand, the chapter will not support either salvation by one's own moral effort or Pharisaic legalism, because the whole appeal is grounded in the character and will of God – his justice and his will to save. Any future that Israel might have flowed from God's grace and longing for life. For them, repentance and regeneration (30f.) must be marked by genuine moral change, which is a fully New Testament principle also. Our evangelism, therefore, to be consistent with God's own desires, must relate to God's will for life on earth, and not just be a matter of making people secure for eternity. That is part of what it means as "Good News". If our evangelism produced people who could be described as righteous in terms of the qualities and behaviour of vs. 5–9 it would indeed be "good news to the poor" in many places.

Individual and Community

Finally, we need to see the balance between individual and

community in the chapter. The chapter is often held up as the
great text for individual responsibility and therefore as a defence
for an individualistic understanding of the Gospel (particularly in
the evangelistic use of vs. 4). However, although the case study is
set up in individual terms, Ezekiel's whole purpose is to move
the community from its self-excusing, God-accusing stance
towards repentance and life. Furthermore, while the challenge is
certainly addressed to individuals, the ethical values and
behaviour which Ezekiel chooses to include in his portrait of
righteousness and its opposite are ones which are primarily social
and relational in effect. This balance of individual and community is addressed further in the Report, Section Two, A.
'Evangelizing Communities'.

JOHN 4
EVANGELISM IN A CONTEXT OF SOCIAL REJECTION

There are three actors in this story: the disciples (collectively),
Jesus, and the woman.

The Disciples

They were not present while Jesus was talking to the woman
because they had gone to buy food (8). We do not know whether
they had gone of their own accord or if Jesus had told them to go
so that he could have some privacy. Certainly they were very
surprised when they came back and found him talking to a
woman (27). Jesus was ignoring all the religious, cultural and
sexual barriers and yet they dared not criticise him.

Instead, perhaps to cover their embarrassment, they preoc-
cupy themselves with food and try to draw Jesus into the same
diversion (31). This is like their misunderstanding after the
feeding of the five thousand, when Jesus spoke of the "leaven of
the Pharisees" and the disciples' minds were still preoccupied
with bread. Like so much of the Church today, they lacked the
vision for the spiritual opportunity that was on Jesus' heart at
this point and could not enter into the urgency of his mission. So
Jesus gives them a mini-lecture on priorities in mission (34–38).
Real work means being committed to obedience to the God who

sends. That is where sustenance is to be found. He also stresses the urgency of the approaching harvest. The work must be finished. Time is short. The workers must co-operate in the task.

The disciples had not begun to grasp all this yet, and perhaps Jesus had sent them off so that he could get on with his task uninterrupted and then let them come in when it was a *fait accompli*. Jesus knew from experience how critical his disciples and others could be of those he chose to reach out to (e.g. Zacchaeus, the woman who anointed him, etc). If they had been present, they would have come up with critical remarks that would have cut the woman off. Women respond differently to men. They are more easily crushed by words and antagonism. But when gripped with the truth in their own experience, nothing can stop them. This Samaritan woman's zeal is matched by the women after the resurrection whom no incredulity and contempt could silence. But the disciples (all men) did not recognise this, and perhaps that's why Jesus sent them away.

Jesus

There is something very beautiful about the way Jesus related to this woman. She was of a different faith, and she was a woman. But Jesus makes the simple request, "Give me a drink". He begins where she is, then gently leads her to where he wants her to be and offers her living water. In reaching women, or people of other faiths, this is very important. We need to understand their situation, fears and longings, before presenting the truth to them.

"Go call your husband!" This draws a curt reply with a touch of defiance. But underneath her bald statement, "I have no husband", lies a lot of pain. What had she gone through, having changed husbands five times? How much had she been used and abused? What social stigma she bore, no longer even legitimately married at all! Yet Jesus did not condemn or criticise her, or call her immoral and turn away. The purpose of his probing was not to drive her further into her shame but to draw her out towards himself and to new hope and life and living water.

When Christians try to reach out to others of different faiths, so often they are full of self-righteousness: "I have what you do not have". They rush in with questions and challenges without any personal relationship or even simple courtesy. Jesus shows such gentleness and courtesy. He talks on equal terms with her. In Asian culture, women have no sense of worth and are rarely treated as persons in their own right. Jesus treats her as a person worth listening to, worth taking time over.

In talking to this Samaritan woman, alone, Jesus was exposing himself to criticism – as he did constantly throughout his ministry. Yet he seems to have been unconcerned about what his disciples or other fellow Jews might have thought about him, socially or morally. He was not concerned about being considered "good" by the standards of his contemporaries. We might add that his behaviour must have exposed him, as a man, to temptation also. Yet his drive to evangelize, his motivation to seek the lost, his urgent desire to be doing his Father's harvest work, were stronger than the risks. We tend to weigh the risks and err on the side of caution. Doubtless there is a place for wisdom and circumspection. But it seems so often that somewhere between temptation and reputation we miss opportunities.

Apart from the moral and social questions, she was also a person from a different theological tradition and background, and one which Jews despised. But Jesus dialogues in reason and gentleness over the issue she raises (20ff). He thus not only avoided producing anger and reinforcing divisions, but also led the conversation towards the crucial recognition of his own identity and significance as the Messiah.

The Woman

If this woman ever came to our church or organization, we would not consider such a person as a possible evangelist. She would be thought the worst candidate for an evangelistic team. But actually she was the best! She went and immediately spread the word. One woman evangelized a whole village and led them to meet Jesus.

Women have a tremendous response. They hunger, thirst, and search for what is real and meaningful, and when they find it, they will give up everything for it. This was so for other women in Jesus' ministry in the Gospels. And after the resurrection, it was a woman again who was the first evangelist – Mary Magdalene, "the apostle to the apostles". For the sake of loved ones, women will go to any lengths. That is what makes them very good evangelists. The history of mission is full of women who have been the first to go to places where men would not, and who have achieved things men never dreamt of. Pandita Ramabai is one outstanding example from India. Part of their evangelistic potential is that people will talk with their hearts to a woman. Women have a ministry with the heart, to the heart.

So this unlikely woman brought a whole village to the Lord. Notice the balance between John's comment: "they believed in him because of the woman's testimony", and the Samaritans' comment "We no longer believe just because of what you said but now we have heard for ourselves" (39, 42). Women often fear that because they are not treated seriously as persons, their words will not be listened to, or have any impact. Here, they did. As a perspective on women's struggle for status, it is liberating to find that my true status and identity is in Christ, no matter what society or men may do to me or think of me. It is that work of grace in my heart first which enables me to reach out to others with confidence.

One person was touched and a whole village was evangelized, because of how closely knit the community was. In communities with extended families, evangelism of one member will often draw in the rest of the extended family. We must never overlook the importance of a single convert. Furthermore, she was the outcast of the village – unable to draw her water in the company of the other women. The very woman who had scandalized the whole community now evangelized the whole community!

It seems to be almost a pattern in the Bible that God lays his hand on colourful and scandalous characters and then changes them and uses them. Paul is another example. How can we make room for that kind of person in our evangelistic strategy? Unfortunately we never find out because we do not even want to associate with such people, evangelistically or otherwise. In India, most Christian women will not work with prostitutes, because of fear of being tarnished with the same stigma. Yet the real scandal in India is that which the churches themselves bring on the name of Christ through their corruption and division. We have more infighting than mission. But that does not stop Christ working. God has his own methods of acting, when the Church gets in the way. Sometimes it seems that, like Jesus in this story, he needs the disciples out of his way before he can really begin to work.

ACTS 3 AND 4
EVANGELISM IN A CONTEXT OF PHYSICAL HEALING

In 1853 a missionary called David Hendra went to Ibadan, Nigeria. Every morning he would go out to visit the sick and help them. One day he went to the house of the parliament chief and after treating the sick he sat down to preach the Gospel and teach about Jesus Christ. A few days later the chief was watching him. At one point, he accidentally hurt a sick woman whom he was treating. She screamed and hit him. Immediately he apologized to her for causing her pain but carried on trying to treat her. Later the chief summoned Hendra and asked him why he had concealed his true identity. Hendra didn't understand until the chief insisted that Hendra himself was the Jesus he had been teaching about. The chief could see no difference between what Hendra had said about Jesus and how he himself behaved, particularly towards a woman, and one who had insulted him.

In this story in Acts we find Jesus still at work in the actions of his followers.

3:1–10.

The first Christians were still observing the Jewish hours of prayer. When communities become Christian, there is no need to throw away what is good in our culture or religious background.

Beggars in the east were accustomed to sit at the entrance to temples and shrines. In many countries they still do. There is an instinctive grasp of the truth that love of God and love of man must go hand in hand. Some may cash in on it and exploit the worshippers, but it is nevertheless a true instinct. It is hard to come to worship God and ignore his creatures in need. It is a constant challenge as to how the Church can fulfil this role without indulging exploiters, the idle, or deliberate dupes. Peter and John transformed the routine expectation of alms into an opportunity for the greater power of Jesus.

3:11–26.

In his message in the temple, Peter was honest and frank in facing the people with what they were responsible for. We should not shrink from confronting people with the reality of sin in their lives and with their responsibility for evil acts. Society crucifies its christs and its criminals, because both make it uncomfortable in opposite ways. But the apostles stressed the vindication of Christ's resurrection. Truth will always triumph over falsehood, love over hatred, good over evil, life over death.

The apostles also stressed the power of the risen Lord, the power of his name. They saw themselves as only channels of that power. They were very aware of their own limitations, but put no limitation on what they could do in the power of the risen Lord. Dependence on "What I can do" produces failure, frustation and fear; but "Not I, but Christ," produces peace and power.

The apostles seized the opportunity of the healing miracle to explain their faith and present the Gospel. Jesus was not merely one who had gone about doing good, but also the conqueror of sin, death and all the forces of evil. His resurrection vindicated him as the Christ, and therefore the expected restoration of Israel and final blessing to the nations in fulfilment of the covenant with Abraham, was already beginning to take place. The urgency of the times called for repentance and a turning back to God in order to enjoy forgiveness and refreshing.

4:1–22.

Here we can see first of all the difference between a good deed and a Christian act. A good deed threatens nobody. It is universally welcomed. But a Christian act is the sign of a new order which God is bringing into being. This is the meaning of John's use of "sign" for the acts of Jesus. Once understood, the action becomes unmistakeable in what it points to.

Peter's act of healing was not just a kindly deed, but a sign of the new order in which people will no longer have to beg for a living. He uses the event to preach the Gospel of God's willingness to save people from any handicap – physical, spiritual and social. At the same time he stresses that the healing was done in and through the name of Jesus, as a vindication of the claim that Jesus was indeed the Messiah, even though he had been rejected and crucified. As such he was the only source of salvation. In the same way Jesus had used his healing of the blind man in John 9 as a basis for his teaching on the Light of the world, and his feeding of the five thousand as a pointer to himself as the Bread of life in John 6.

Secondly, we can see the courage of Peter and John. What they said in explanation was not what the authorities wanted to hear. The Sanhedrin was the highest court, the same as had condemned Jesus. So Peter and John knew their lives were at stake. Yet they showed cool courage. Evangelism involves risk, not only for expatriate missionaries, but for national Christians under threat from political and other forms of opposition. The enemies of the cross used two weapons: contempt and threat. But the apostles' answer used the weapon of unanswerable fact. "You crucified Jesus. But God has raised him. And it is in his name that this healing has taken place". This courage was founded on loyalty to God and their personal experience of Christ (19f.).

4:23–37.

The response of the church was both prayerful and practical. The apostles needed courage, so they gathered the believers to pray with them and for them. Likewise, any of us involved in mission need faith, courage and prayer. Only thus can we operate, like the apostles, in the power of the Holy Spirit. The result of the prayer meeting was not only that the apostles were strengthened, but that *all the believers* were enabled to speak the word boldly (31).

Significantly, however, the early Church was not so preoccupied with prayer and preaching that they neglected practical love and care of the needy. So Luke ends the whole incident in the same way it had begun, with practical, caring love exercised in the name of Christ. Though it was spontaneous and not organized by a committee, Luke sees it just as much as a sign of the new age of fulfilment in the power of the Spirit as the preaching of the Gospel itself. This is clear from the way verse 34 quotes Deuteronomy 15:4 which had promised "there will be no needy people among you", if only Israel would obey God. The same pattern is found in Acts 2, where the account of apostolic preaching is immediately followed by the description of the practical economic sharing of the believers (2:42–47). It is clearly Luke's intention to show that the rapid growth of the early Church was related not only to the evangelistic preaching and courageous witness of the apostles, but to the radical new quality of community life being demonstrated by ordinary believers.

Chapter Five

Guidelines for preparing a case study

Introduction

These guidelines are only intended to help you share your experience with the rest of the participants in such a way as to facilitate critical and theological reflection. The purpose of the structure is not to straitjacket everything, but to enable us to make constructive comparisons and draw maximum benefit from the material and personal resources at the consultation. The headings highlight some of the important aspects that we would like you to share with us. You may wish to answer the questions more or less as set out here, or you may prefer a different style of presenting your experience and thoughts. Please feel free also to supplement your case study with any other material, photographs, leaflets, cuttings, etc.

I Context

Describe as succinctly as possible the context of your evangelism: the type of people, social situation, economic situation, political and cultural background, factors favourable or unfavourable to evangelism, etc.

II History

Record something of the history of your work: your recollections of when your ministry started, whether you started it or entered into the labours of others before you (in which case give brief historical details prior to your own involvement), the key persons, the hurdles and encouragements, the challenges and fears, the compelling reasons for beginning the work, the stages of progress, ups and downs, the developing structures and relationships with other bodies or churches. What were the goals of your work initially? Have they changed or been achieved?

III Indicators

What are the indicators used in your ministry or project by which you measure the effectiveness of the evangelistic activity? e.g.

Awareness of the name of Jesus Christ
Change in attitude towards Jesus Christ
Acknowledging Jesus Christ as the only God
Change in attitudes, behaviour and relationships
Change in the social patterns of the whole community
Ability to share Jesus with others
Birth and growth of a church etc?

IV Methods

A major purpose of our consultation is to learn from differing methods and to reflect on them theologically, so please try to be as specific as possible in describing the "how" of your evangelism. Do you use a single main method, or multi-methods? How does your method relate to the context? Have you changed your method in the course of time and if so, for what reasons and with what results? Are there any social, economic or political dimensions to your ministry? Are your methods significantly different from those of any other group or church or mission agency which is working evangelistically in the same context? If so, why?

V Message

What is the essence of the gospel as presented in your evangelistic ministry? Is there any particular aspect of the gospel which forms the major focus of your evangelism because of the specific context in which you work? Have you found that your emphasis has changed over the years? Has your own understanding of the gospel changed in the course of your ministry? If so, has this been because of theological reflection or engagement in your context? What biblical themes are to the fore in your work?

VI Effect

Give some assessment of the results of your ministry or project. What is its impact on the wider community and on the church? In many cases where evangelism is integrated with social action one of the effects is a definite change in the quality of life in the community. In other cases, however, the combination of evangelistic and social ministries is suspected of producing Christians for economic benefits. What is your experience?

Sometimes evangelism produces Christian communities who are socially docile with no concern for the needs of their context. Sometimes it produces an increased level of practical involvement. Again, what is your experience?

Can you describe the effect of your ministry of evangelism upon yourself, your co-workers, or the church which supports you in the ministry?

VII Discipleship and the church

What kind of Christians have been produced through your ministry or project? What kind of practical Christian discipleship has emerged? What kind of churches have been planted – in terms of leadership, membership, dependence or independence, socially active or passive, evangelistically involved or not, etc?

VIII Resistance

How has the community responded to evangelism in their midst? Initially? In the longer term? Are there major constraints upon your work – e.g. from other faiths, a resistant culture, political or legal restrictions, etc? How have they been faced?

Please feel free to add a number of questions or issues, either to challenge other participants in their interaction with what you present, or seeking theological or practical help from others in the areas that concern you.

Chapter Six

Nigeria: The local church and the Bishop in Evangelism

Emmanuel B. Gbonigi

Context

Nigeria has been under a chronic economic burden for some time. The vast mineral resources with which the country is endowed by God, which ought to have been a catalyst to its being a great nation in terms of wealth have been grossly mismanaged by succeeding governments both civilian and military. This invariably has left the teaming masses impoverished. Consequently, many are turning to God through Jesus Christ, Allah, or gods or a mixture of more than one of these, for their economic survival.

In addition, a growing wave of cultural revival as the only solution to our economic, political, and social morass compounds the already confused atmosphere. This leaves a large segment of the populace with syncretistic ideas, confused minds, an ignorant outlook, and a non-committal stance to the expectations of a Christian disciple.

In this situation socialists and communists capitalise on the seeming ineptitude of the democratic world to redeem the country from the depth of woes to which it has been plunged. They are quick to point out, as is often the case, that religion is just an 'opium of the people'; that God has no hand in the redemption of man and that man is his own god and redeemer. Current events in the Communist world are proving that this assertion is false.

On the other hand, the advocates of traditional religion, which is mainly idol worship, counsel a return to the gods and practices of our forefathers. Sacrifices to appease various deities for different purposes abound. Many ordinary church-goers have found themselves caught in the web of some of these rituals. To assuage their guilty feelings they often say 'Igbagbo ko ni ki a ma se oro ile eni' meaning 'Faith does not forbid a Christian from participating in the worship of his or her clan deity.'

These people are mainly those who, having undergone the rites of the Church viz: baptism, confirmation or even ordination have a wrong notion that their tickets to heaven have been secured and the need for personal commitment to Jesus and his teachings become secondary. They are like the Jews who, according to Jesus, used to boast of having Abraham as their father, as if the faith of Abraham alone was what was required for their salvation.

Others have experienced the new birth but have remained perpetual babies. They know the Lord Jesus, but nothing beyond this infantile knowledge. They are yet to mature into the stature of disciples – living evangelists and witnesses.

We, however, thank God for the minority group, a kind of remnant of committed and zealous Christians who are actively involved, one way or the other, in evangelism. In order to do effective evangelism, especially in the local church, all the problems enumerated above have to be tackled and the available resources as outlined in the paragraph above harnessed.

History

My primary assignment as a church leader is to lead people to the Lord Jesus Christ, and stimulate the growth of those who already know him. This task cannot be seen as accomplished until a convert or believer is nurtured to maturity; he or she is able not just to stand alone, but to bring others and take them through the cycle he has gone through. I have seen many in my position who, over the years, have been reduced to mere administrative heads. This is a subtle attack of the evil one to render ineffective an erstwhile zealous believer and pastor.

One of the ways in which I have tried to maintain my spiritual alertness is to collaborate actively with other bodies who share the same vision and goals with me – bodies like the Evangelical Fellowship in Anglican Communion (EFAC), Scripture Union, Operation Good News, Campus Crusade for Christ or Great Commission Movement, Consultation AD 2000, 'Here's Life' Programme, Calvary Productions, to mention a few. I encourage some of my pastors with like minds to rub minds together with members of these bodies. We try to be open to new ideas provided they are grounded in the scriptures.

My initial goal was to ensure that those who bear the name of Christ are seen to be doing what their calling entails, and that the pastors are equipped to teach, preach and heal. This goal will be discussed further in the methodology section.

I have had to change from one approach to another in order to ensure greater effectiveness.

Indicators

The indicators by which I measure the effectiveness of evangelistic activity have been:

1 Awareness of the name of Jesus Christ as being greater than any other name.
2 Return of the youths to a full participation in the various church activities.
3 Feedback from the participants and those who come under the evangelical thrust.
4 Change in attitude, behaviour and relationships especially to Jesus Christ and his Gospel.
5 Willingness and ability to share Jesus with others.
6 Change in social patterns of the local church used as a case study.

Methods and Message

At the beginning of this experiment, I set up a Missionary Board charged with the responsibility of evangelism within our diocese. Part of their terms of reference was to study and appraise situations, viz: Christian awareness within our Diocese, and to plan towards taking Christ to all people. Some evangelical outreaches were planned at some locations and at sundry times. But I found that the impact on the people was not very significant, and did not last long. The evangelists did not spend enough time the people to make any reasonable impact on them.

I was quite concerned about this and had to seek the face of the Lord for further guidance. The Lord heard our prayer and there

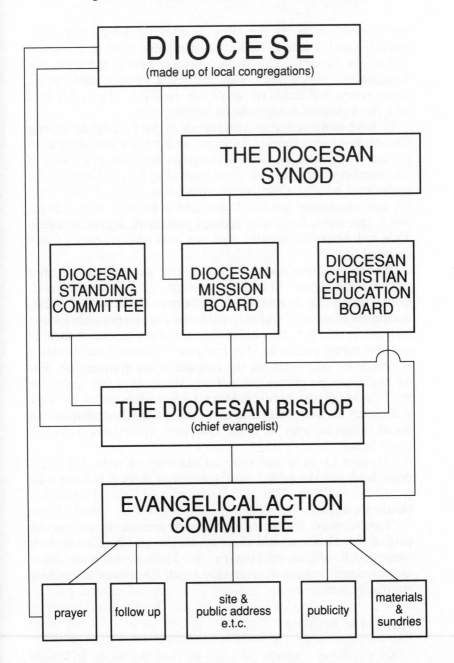

was a fresh vision for the same mission. In 1986, during the annual Synod, I had an indication that there must be a renewal within the Church. The theme for the Synod that year was 'Renewal of the Church'. This marked a turning point in the entire evangelical thrust within our diocese. Part of what I shared with the delegates is reproduced below:

"I have observed that syncretism is very rampant among Christians in our country at large, and within our diocese in particular. The first and second commandments seem to many of our members mere precepts to be learned and reproduced for the purpose of passing their confirmation test. To such members, the commandments are not divine laws to be believed and lived. They, therefore, freely and actively participate in idol worship. This sad situation dictates that we seek the renewal of our spiritual life.

"So far, we have had two civilian and five military regimes since Independence. In addition, we have had six coups d'etat. Consequently, we as a nation, have been in a state of instability. A number of internal and external factors are responsible for our instability; we, however, know that the most serious of them is our low moral standard. Our low moral standard constitutes a challenge for us to seek for the renewal of our spiritual life. For we know that we cannot live as God intends us to live unless we are first of all the kind of persons he intends us to be. Our sufficiency for holy living is in God: and it is in Christ that we can do all things because he is the One who strengthens us in our inner being.

"Another factor is our spiritual maturity or lack of it. This point is closely connected with syncretism since it is those who would not enthrone God in their hearts and lives who worship inanimate objects.

"Furthermore, the current upsurge of evangelistic zeal on the part of the Muslims, and their onslaught on Christianity with considerable official backing by the Federal and some State Governments, constitute a reveille to all Christians to be fully spiritually armed.

Concept of Renewal

"The Christian concept of renewal has its basis in God's outpouring of his Spirit who restores his people to normal spiritual life after a period of corporate declension. This trend permeates the Old Testament. Ezekiel's vision of the valley of dry bones followed by the revival of worship after Israel's return from Babylonian exile is a classic example of this divine act.

"Periods of spiritual decline occur in history because the gravity of indwelling sin keeps pulling believers first into formal religion and then into open apostasy. Periods of awakening alternate with these as God graciously breathes new life into his people.

"You have professed faith in Jesus Christ. You have been baptized and confirmed. Those of you in the House of Clergy have been ordained. All of you hold certain offices in the Church, including membership of the Parish Council or Standing Committee, and the Diocesan Synod. So, outwardly and here on earth you are seen to belong to the New Israel, the Household of Faith, the Kingdom of God. But are you sure you are a citizen of God's Kingdom in the spiritual sense?

Have you been born again?

Have you totally renounced all forms of idol worship?

Have you yielded undivided, unconditional and thankful obedience to God?"

These words must have come as a rude shock to many but the bad good news about one's condition, before Christ takes his rightful place of ownership and control, has to be clearly stated. It is after this that one can appropriate the "goodies" in the good news about sonship, regeneration, and discipleship.

I also identified with the Christians' resistance to the gradual suppression of the faith by militant Muslims. This earned me a lot of displeasure from those who benefit materially and otherwise from the "status quo". But it was helpful in awakening many who were asleep. By and large an awareness to be evangelized and to evangelize was created in the minds of the people.

I took advantage of this and followed it up with systematic training of the clergy. This process is still going on and has had a lot of impact on the pulpit ministry. I realized that much impact on the pulpit ministry could be achieved if the laity were actively involved in evangelism and encouraged to play a leading role.

Towards this end, a training programme was organized on a parish basis, using among others the Great Commission Movement's material on the Basic Course and Message Workbook. Each willing participant was taken through a series of teaching from 'Salvation' to 'Living a Successful Christian and Witnessing Life'. The trained people are now given responsibility on an individual and church group basis to evangelize within their community. In addition, these people are encouraged to avail the local churches of their services. This is gradually having a good effect on the church sub-groups.

This latter approach to evangelism is a bit different from the norm, that is, radio and television evangelism, and the organisation of large crusades or rallies, or open-air preaching. Every participant in the group is a soul winner, and is committed to the task because his Master demands it. This type of spirit hardly gives up because it is always faced with challenges on a daily basis. The whole Gospel is expected to change the person in all areas of life. Those who respond to be the mouthpiece of the Lord Jesus have also identified (empathised) with the social needs of the people. On many occasions these needs far outweigh the available resources. This brings quite a heavy burden on the church purse, and consequently on the membership. However, God is always faithful to ensure that our needs are provided for.

Effect

The effect of this project has been overwhelming. Some of the participants have said:

> "I had always believed that the job of witnessing is for the clerics and my responsibility is to be a good listener. But now, I know better; that we are supposed to be workers in the same vineyard. When he plants, I water, and when I plant he waters." (A 50 year old woman participant).

> "Prior to this time (of training), none of us would want to share our faith with others because some pastors would feel envious and may even accuse us of wanting to take their job. However, things are different now. The fact that the Bishop is behind this training gives us the boldness to be what we are – saved and trained to be soul winners."

> "I had written off the Church (a particular church in the community) for quite some time. But, the fact that people come

from within that same place to share the Gospel with me is giving me second thoughts."

"It is exciting having to lead someone to the Lord after more than two decades of being a believer."

"My life cannot be the same again, after finding this secret of witnessing."

"Please ensure that you extend this training and challenge to other churches."

In the present experience, there has not been any major thrust on the social side of the ministry.

Resistance

The community has been generally responsive to evangelism. On many occasions, requests have been made for more visits by the evangelists. However, in a few cases, some resistance was encountered from die-hard traditionalists and Muslims. During one of our door-to-door witnessing sessions, some traditionalists openly cursed the evangelists and threatened them with "juju", black magic or witch craft. But we all rejoiced because of the rare privilege of suffering for the Lord (Philippians 1:9).

Muslims generally are interested in argument. But a few often listen, while some make decisions for the Lord. In the secondary schools, however, the experience is different, especially in Federal Government Institutions. There is an unwritten law that pupils cannot change their "religion" while at government schools. So do we stop preaching to non-Christians? God forbid. We still preach and converts are made. Christians organize religious activities in the schools. The students are encouraged to study the scriptures and grow. Since the young people are forbidden to convert while under the authority of their parents, we refrain from baptizing them while they are still in school, although they may attend all the baptismal classes.

Chapter Seven

Kenya: Evangelism among Nomadic Communities

David Gitari

Introduction

The peoples of Northern Kenya whom we are trying to reach with the Gospel of Jesus Christ are basically nomadic. The Boran, the Gabbra and the Rendille of Marsabit District are mobile peoples. They build temporary houses, and after pasturing their cows, goats and camels in the area for a few weeks, they are on the move again in search of fresh grazing and water. Their life revolves around the search for water and grass for their animals. This way of life is very similar to that of the Maasai, the best-known nomadic people of Kenya and Tanzania.

The Gospel and Traditional Culture

We are not sentimental admirers of traditional cultures. Sometimes the Gospel frankly opposes the cherished beliefs of a people. The Maasai, for example, believe that all the cattle in the world belong to them, and that they are the one and only people in the world endowed by God with the grace of owning cattle. Consequently in Maasai traditional belief, any cattle currently being kept by other tribes are in the wrong hands. If Maasai warriors march into the territory of the neighbouring WaKamba tribe to capture the WaKamba's cattle, this is not seen as stealing; it is merely retrieving the cattle and returning them to their rightful home. Jesus, the judge of culture, must visit the Maasai and tell them: "You have heard it was said of old, 'All cattle belong to the Maasai, and that to take WaKamba cattle is not stealing'. But I say to you, 'If you love the WaKamba, do not take their cattle'."

In our approach to the nomadic people of Northern Kenya we are very much aware that the Gospel cannot tolerate some aspects of their culture. In the Gabbra culture, if a woman gives birth to twins, the two children must be killed, as the birth of twins is considered a bad omen. Our evangelists among the Gabbra have made it very clear that even twins are made in God's image and we must not destroy life created by God himself.

So the Gospel became good news to a certain Gabbra lady called Sara. She gave birth to twins in 1978, and the first Gabbra Anglican priest, Revd Andrew Adano, together with the local Roman Catholic father, marshalled all their efforts to ensure that the twins were not destroyed. Hence if the culture says "Kill the twins", the good news of the gospel declares "Thou shalt not kill". In our evangelism among the Gabbra we do not hesitate to remind them of those cultural practices which are contrary to the Gospel of Christ.

The Gospel to Communities

One of the most important aspects of African culture which the Gospel affirms is the African understanding of humanity. Although an individual has his own unique personality, Dr John Mbiti is right to say that in African thought the individual is fully a person only in the context of the community: "The individual can only say: 'I am, because we are; and since we are, therefore I am.' "[1]

We have inherited from the western Church a concept of evangelism as winning individuals to Jesus Christ. Each person has individually to accept Christ as a personal saviour. But an individual making a major decision in his life alone is alien to African culture. When a young person wishes to get married, the decision is so important that the whole family and indeed the entire clan has to be involved. Making a decision to follow Christ can also be said to be so important that it should not be left to an individual.[2] We are convinced that in our primary evangelism among these nomadic peoples, our approach must not be that of rescuing individuals from a sinking boat, but rather winning communities to Jesus Christ.

The publication of *Christianity Rediscovered*[3] by Vincent Donovan has been a great inspiration to us in community evangelism. Donovan was a Roman Catholic missionary among the Maasai of Northern Tanzania. He was disillusioned by the

failure of the methods used by his church to evangelize the
Maasai. For many years the Church's strategy had been to lure
Maasai children to join mission boarding schools, where they
were indoctrinated with Christianity, in the hope that they would
go back to their parents and tell them about Christ. But,
according to Donovan, 'no Catholic child on leaving school has
continued to practice his religion'; for the integrity of Maasai
society proved too strong and cohesive to be subverted in this
fashion. Donovan proposed to his bishop that he be allowed to go
to the Maasai villages and talk to the people about Christ,
without any material benefits in his hand. This was a radical
departure from the traditional procedure of evangelizing by
building schools and hospitals.

Donovan started visiting six Maasai manyattas, where he
requested the chief of each manyatta to gather people together at
least once a week so that he could tell them about God. Over
several months he would meet the people early in the morning,
before they went out to pasture their cattle. As he shared the
Gospel with them, he found to his surprise that they were very
willing to listen. When he had told them all that he wanted to tell
them about Jesus Christ, he challenged them to decide whether
they wanted to become Christians and be baptized or not. He left
them for a while to think about this challenge as a community.
When he returned, five out of the six communities had decided
to become Christians and to be baptized.

Donovan observed that some people in each village had not
attended his classes. He told the elders that he could not baptize
such people. However, the elders told him, 'You either baptize
all of us or none of us, for we refuse to be divided. These people
whom you say did not attend classes, were absent because we had
sent them away. But each evening we told them all that you had
taught us.' Donovan, realizing the strength of the community
ties, baptized entire communities. The community leaders spoke
on behalf of everyone, and their authority and decision was
acceptable to all.

To make an individualistic appeal to a Rendille or Boran
community, asking people to accept Christ one by one, may be
contrary to the Gospel. St Paul preached and baptized in the
household of Cornelius, and in that of the Philippian jailer. The
Gospel can also be preached in the household of a nomadic
people, respecting and preserving their traditional communita-

rian culture. In our evangelism in Northern Kenya, we are taking seriously the idea of community evangelism. We are not evangelizing individuals to pluck them out of their communities; but after a period of instruction, communities are turning to Christ, and are being baptized and incorporated into the life of the Church.

Missionaries have been at work in Northern Kenya for many years. However, rapid numerical growth is a much more recent phenomenon. The breakthrough among the Gabbra began in 1977 when we ordained the Revd Andrew Adano as the first Gabbra priest and bought him a camel, a mule and forty goats. The work among the Turkana of Isiolo district began in 1981.

The vicar of the parish began to visit the Turkana and Samburu people in their manyattas, and presented the Gospel to the community as a whole. The vicar would make repeated visits to a certain manyatta, taking care to meet the people and to learn their customs and social courtesies. At the end of the visit the vicar would call a meeting and invite a respected elder of the manyatta to begin the proceedings with a traditional prayer. The vicar would then explain some aspect of the Christian message. He always began with common ground with traditional Turkana/ Samburu religion: for example God as Creator and Sustainer. In later meetings he would move on to present Jesus as the Son of this God, who was born and lived on earth, and became the saviour. He would explain how sin arose, and how Jesus could deliver people from sin.

The hearers had plenty of questions: Who exactly was this Jesus? What did he look like? If he was the Son of God the Provider, how could he help them when they were suffering from sickness and the effects of drought? The vicar did his best to answer the questions, invited the elder to close with further prayer, and bade his hearers farewell.

After several months, some members of the manyatta – perhaps five out of a group of twenty adults – would be ready for baptism. Unlike Donovan, the vicars of Isiolo did not ask for a purely communal response. Nevertheless, experience showed that soon after the initial baptisms of those who seemed most ready, other members of the manyatta would also come forward to declare their allegiance to Christ. In this way whole manyattas would be added to the Church, and rapid numerical growth began.

In 1985 we baptized 180 Turkana Christians in one service at Epiding; and a few months later 257 more were baptized. Our work among the Rendille began in 1986, when an entire community of 100 Rendille people at Ula Ula turned to Christ and were baptized, together with their chief. Another community of 500 Rendille people at Kargi began to turn to Christ early in 1988. As a result of the devoted work of the evangelists, we are starting an average of two new congregations a month, most of them under trees.

Several factors contributed to this achievement. One was the humility of successive vicars in setting aside their own Kikuyu culture and presenting the Gospel in terms meaningful to Turkanas and Samburus. Another was their flexibility in allowing converts to develop new forms of Christian prayer and worship in line with their own traditions, rather than insisting on Prayer Book worship. A third factor was the self-reliance and responsibility which the converts were expected to show from the first: as elders of the new congregations and also in devising and implementing self-help projects, for example starting adult literacy programmes. Finally there was the goodwill resulting from the Diocese's practical care for the people of Isiolo, whether Christian or not; especially during the disastrous drought of 1984, when food supplies and goats for restocking were distributed by the Diocese.

In 1 Corinthians 9.22b -23, Paul describes his approach to evangelism: "I have become all things to all men, that I might by all means save some." In our primary evangelism in Northern Kenya, we have realized that we cannot be effective unless we are willing to become 'Gabbras to the Gabbra, and Rendilles to the Rendille', so that we may share the blessings of the Gospel with them.

Appropriate Evangelism

We are seeking to apply the great missionary principles of Henry Venn and Roland Allen, and create a church which is 'self-supporting, self-governing and self-propagating'. At this early stage the evangelists still need the external support supplied by the Diocesan Missionary Association: the Association encourages Christians in other parts of the Diocese to participate in primary evangelism in Northern Kenya by prayerful support of the work. However, the actual work of primary evangelism among the Gabbra is being done by the Gabbra themselves.

The techniques of evangelism used must be appropriate. In evangelism among the Gabbra, this begins with the evangelist's lifestyle. Gabbra communities are camel nomads; they use their camels both to fetch water and also to carry house and household goods when the time comes to move on. Revd Andrew Adano and the five evangelists working among the Gabbra under him have five camels being used in evangelism. The evangelists live among the Gabbra, participating in the activities of communal life, travelling with their camels to search for water, joining the caravans in search of new grazing areas.

The evangelist's message must also be delivered in an appropriate setting. It is while travelling or watering animals that the evangelists tell their fellow Gabbras about the Lord Jesus Christ. In the evenings the community gathers around the evangelists and the Gospel is presented to them. The evangelist does not give a lengthy monologue, but rather he invites his hearers to join a dialogue, and so the Gospel of Jesus Christ is presented to the whole community.

The focus of the message must also be appropriate. The evangelist begins with the traditional Gabbra concept of God, and seeks to enrich it with the understanding of what God has done in Christ Jesus. The words of the writer to the Hebrews become good news to these mobile people: "In many and various ways God spoke of old to our fathers by the prophets; but in these last days he has spoken to us by a Son."

The evangelist must also invite an appropriate response to the message. When he is satisfied that the community clearly understands the Gospel, he invites the whole manyatta to take a decision to follow Christ or not. The elders meet to discuss that challenge, and if they decide to accept Christianity, then the whole community is baptized.

From the beginning, the new Christian community must adopt appropriate practices. Baptismal technique is a case in point: with so little water available in this semi-desert area, baptism by sprinkling is the most sensible way to baptize. Again, it is no use suggesting that the community should build themselves a church building, since they will soon be on the move again. This is a mobile Church. The camel caravans of

Gabbra Christians search for new grazing areas as before; but now they are also pilgrims like Abraham, who ' . . .went out, not knowing where he was to go. By faith he sojourned in the land of promise, as in a foreign land, living in tents . . . For people who speak thus make it clear that they are seeking a homeland.' (Hebrews 11. 8–14).

In worship we want the emerging mobile churches in Northern Kenya to make full use of the traditional ways of saying prayers where the worshippers respond to every sentence said by the leader. We are reluctant to impose on them a translation of the 1662 prayer book.[4]

Evangelism and Social Reponsibility

We have been inspired by the example and testimony of Father Vincent Donovan's work among the Maasai. Nevertheless in one very important respect, our approach diverges from his.

Donovan was working in a context in which for many years development activities such as building schools and hospitals had been substituted for preaching and evangelism. This had created confusion among the Maasai, who thought that these activities were all that Christianity contained. Donovan's task was to disclose the story of the life, death and resurrection of Jesus Christ, and the news that in Christ God has acted to save people. Donovan found it necessary to cut himself off from development activities and concentrate on preaching.

When we began our ministry in Northern Kenya we did not face Donovan's problems of previous misleading examples. Consequently we were free to proclaim the Gospel in its holistic richness from the first. We are carrying out programmes for community health education and livestock development as well as feeding the hungry. We are also interested in issues of justice and peace as they arise.

There is no question of regarding evangelism as primary and seeing our social responsibility as secondary in our mission to the people of Northern Kenya. These nomadic peoples are faced with the implications of climatic change which resulted in a series of disastrous droughts in recent years. They are also struggling with man-made changes. Rising population caused by reduced mortality, and unsatisfactory patterns of grazing caused by the digging of wells. We have a saying that ' a hungry stomach has no ears.' We cannot preach first and then feed people afterwards. The man who was ill for thirty-eight years was healed by Jesus first with the words 'Rise, take up your pallet and walk' (John 5:8). Only at a later meeting did Jesus 'evangelize' him with the words 'See, you are well! Sin no more, that nothing worse befall you' (John 5:14). We have refused to put a wedge between evangelism and socio-political responsibility.[5] We believe that this approach is required by obedience to the Great Commission and to the Great Commandment.

Naturally it is vital that our social activity is carried out in an appropriate manner, just as much as our evangelism. In an earlier paper I wrote of the 'Feed me' mentality:

"If our efforts to help the poor make them dependent on us, then we have not liberated them. Canaan Banana, the president of Zimbabwe, makes this point convincingly when he says: 'The dynamics of being poor are such that the oppressed poor finally accept the inhumanity and humiliation of their situation. They accept the status quo as the normal course of life. Thus to be poor becomes both the state of things and an attitude to life, an outlook and even a world view. The vicious circle is completed when the oppressor in turn internalizes an attitude of permanent supremacy and paternalism towards the poor and undertakes to speak, think and act on behalf of the poor. The poor are thus made dependent and made to feel dependent on the rich.' We thus do not liberate the poor by merely giving them their daily bread. This can also dehumanize them, when they have daily to queue so as to be served with porridge. We must work together with them in seeking ways and means of achieving self-sufficiency. We must go to the very roots of the cause of hunger and poverty."[6]

Conclusion

As the Church in Africa enters the last decade of the twentieth century it must humbly accept the challenge of our Lord Jesus Christ who, seeing how the masses of the people were harassed and helpless like sheep without a shepherd, told his disciples: "The harvest is plentiful but the labourers are few; pray therefore the Lord of the harvest to send out labourers into his harvest." (Matt. 9.38).

And if the Church is to grow, the labourers who go to the Lord's vineyard must themselves be men and women who have encountered Jesus Christ as Lord and Saviour, and who go to evangelize with a conviction that they are the ambassadors of Jesus Christ. 'To evangelize is to spread the good news that Jesus Christ died for our sins and was raised from the dead according to the scriptures, and that as the reigning Lord he now offers forgiveness of sins, and the liberating gift of the Spirit to all who repent and believe.' This is the simple Gospel proclaimed by our evangelists. They are men and women of comparativelty little education, but their conviction of the uniqueness of the Christ they proclaim, and of his liberating power is so deep and firm that whoever hears the proclamation for the first time, would like to hear more.

Evangelism, then, is the proclamation of the historical, biblical Christ as Saviour and Lord with a view to persuading people to turn to him and be reconciled with him. Models of evangelism are many, but I have attempted to share a model which could be described as 'Incarnational'. It is based on the perception that Jesus 'emptied himself' and chose to 'become flesh' and to 'live among us'. By entering on the stage of human history, he was able to identify himself with humanity and to reveal God and to serve mankind. The Incarnational Model of evangelism demands our Christian presence in the world so that we may be able to share Jesus Christ with the people and communities we encounter. The Incarnational Model also invites us to proclaim the Gospel not from a distance, but rather by penetrating communities and cultures. In the process of this penetration, the customs of the community and culture are either endorsed, challenged or transformed by the Gospel. In this way we believe we are obeying the Great Commission, and as a result ' The Lord is adding to our numbers those who are being saved' and the Church of Christ is growing.[7]

Footnotes

1. J.S.Mbiti, *African Religions and Philosophy* (London, Heinemann, 1969), p.108–109.

2. Dr James I. Packer, writing as an evangelical English scholar for his fellow white English evangelicals, offers the following critique of individualism:

"An atomic individualism, really a product of European rationalism and romanticism two centuries ago, has crept into our thinking about individuals before God, making us unable, it seems, to take seriously the family . . . national and Adamic solidarities which scripture affirms as part of the created order, and which the so-called 'primitive' mind grasps so much better than most of us.' J.I. Packer, 'The Gospel, its content and communication – a theological perspective" in J.R.W. Stott and R. Coote (eds), *Down to Earth* (Grand Rapids, Eerdmans, 1980) p. 102.

3. Vincent Donovan *Christianity Rediscovered* (London, S.C.M., 1978).

4. For example, an ancient litany of the Turkana people has been adapted and used as part of the new *Kenyan Service of Holy Communion* (Nairobi, UZIMA Press, 1990). Traditionally with the dramatic sweeping of their arms, they sent all their problems, difficulties and the devil's works to their enemies, the Maasai or Karamajong. This curse has now been Christianised, but the congregation still accompany it first with a sweep of their arms to the cross behind the holy table and then with the raising of their hands towards heaven.

Minister: All our problems
People: We send to the cross of Christ
Minister: All our difficulties
People: We send to the cross of Christ
Minister: All the devil's works
People: We send to the cross of Christ
Minister: All our hopes
People: We set on the risen Christ.

5. The Lausanne Covenant states: 'We affirm that God is both the Creator and the Judge of all men. We therefore should share his concern for justice and reconciliation throughout human society and for the liberation of men from every kind of oppression. Because mankind is made in the image of God, every person, regardless of race, religion, colour, culture, class, sex or age, has an intrinsic dignity because of which he should be respected and served, not exploited. Here too we express penitence both for our neglect and for having sometimes regarded evangelism and social concern as mutually exclusive. Although reconciliation with man is not reconciliation with God, nor is social action evangelism, nor is political liberation salvation, nevertheless we affirm that evangelism and socio-political involvement are both part of our Christian duty. For both are necessary expressions of our doctrines of God and man, our love for our neighbour and our obedience to Jesus Christ. The message of salvation implies also a message of judgement upon every form of alienation. oppression and discrimination, and we should not be afraid to denounce evil and injustice wherever they exist. When people receive Christ they are born again into his kingdom and must seek not only to exhibit but also to spread its righteousness in the midst of an unrighteous world. The salvation we claim should be transforming us in the totality of our personal and social responsibilities. Faith without works is dead'.

6. D.M. Gitari, 'The Claims of Jesus in the African Context' , in W.M. Lazareth (ed.), *The Lord of Life* (Geneva, W.C.C., 1983) p.47.

7. This case-study was part of a presentation made at the Lambeth Conference of Bishops in 1988. The whole presentation is published in *Proclaiming Christ in Christ's Way* edited by Vinay Samuel and Albrecht Hauser (Oxford, Regnum, 1989). The case-study is also available on video "To Canterbury with a Camel", available from CMS, 157 Waterloo Road, London SE1, and as part of the video "Seeing People through the Eyes of Jesus", three case studies on social concern and evangelisation from India, Peru and Kenya, available from Scripture Union, 130 City Road, London EC1.

Chapter Eight

South Africa: Evangelism in a rural Diocese

Philip LeFeuvre

The Diocese

The Diocese of St. Mark the Evangelist, Pietermaritzburg, is the most northerly diocese in the Republic of South Africa. It covers the areas of the Far Northern Transvaal within the curve of South Africa's borders with Botswana, Zimbabwe and Mozambique. It is the most unevangelized part of South Africa. There are more unevangelized and unreached peoples within the diocese than in the whole of the rest of South Africa put together.

The diocese is less than three years old. Previously it was part of the vast Diocese of Pretoria, and this is undoubtedly part of the Anglican excuse for the unevangelized nature of the areas. Inevitably Church activity tended to centre around the big city and amongst the mines which exist in the southern half of the undivided diocese. Consequently the north was virtually totally neglected. The very reason for the creation of a new diocese was to rectify this imbalance. It became clear that the north would continue to be a Cinderella until it had a centre of jurisdiction within itself.

Context

The heterogeneous nature of the population is indicated by the fact that seven different languages are spoken in the Diocese. The dominant language is North Sotho and 51% of the North Sotho people are Christianised. Under the government's apartheid policy, they live in a self-governing homeland, but one which has refused consistently to take full independence. The homeland, Lebowa, suffers heavily under the migratory labour policy, and most of the men of working age are away in the larger cities. However, a sizeable civil service has been created by the nature of a self-governing system, and so there are a fair number of men connected either with bureaucracy or the professions. There are others who are dependent for their livelihood on employment in the white towns which are to be found up and down the main roads of the Diocese.

At the other end of the spectrum there are the Shangaans, who have shown a resistance to the Gospel, who also live in a self-governing bantustan, and who are less than 20% Christianised. In this area the work of the Diocese is weak in that we have nobody who can speak the Shangaan language. The so-called independent Republic of Venda also lies within the Diocese. Here too there has been resistance to the Gospel. Christianisation is at about 20%.

All these areas have vast numbers of young people of school-going age, and also large numbers of women, particularly elderly women. But the real manpower is absent in the cities. This is a very important factor to bear in mind in seeking to establish Christian mission, to plant churches, and to identify direction of ministry. Clearly a maximum outreach has to be directed towards children and young people, both in the somewhat fractured home situation and through the schools and churches.

The economic context is that of a Two-Thirds World, rural society. There is no starvation in the area and even malnutrition is minimal. But, while there is very little grinding proverty, most people do battle to make ends meet. A great deal of the money in circulation is imported via the salaries and by the menfolk in the cities. A lot of subsistence farming is done, but the area is prone to drought. The existence of relatively wealthy white communities dotted around the Diocese also helps to keep money in circulation in the rural areas.

Usually alongside the white towns are black towns which are basically reservoirs of labour for white commerce, industry and domestic service. In these black towns, the black people are becoming increasingly politicized, but not to the extent that is found in a large cities. This politicization has tended to be disadvantageous to mission and evangelism as most of the young people – usually with some justification – believe that the churches have not really come to grips with the basic political and economic issues of the country.

In other places, resistance to the Gospel has been as a result of the deep seated traditional patterns, and this has been reinforced by the creation of highly syncretistic religious groupings which fall generally under the title of African Independent Churches. The area covered by this Diocese is dominated by one in particular, the Zion Christian Church. This has millions of adherents, claims to follow Christ, but places its own founder on the same level as a mediator. The strength of the Z.C.C. has been in its ability to incorporate a whole host of traditional beliefs, many of which are totally unscriptural and, therefore, unacceptable to orthodox Christianity.

Indicators

The indicators which we use most consistently across the Diocese to measure the effectiveness of evangelistic activity are worship, witness and giving. These can be applied both individually and corporately, but it is on the latter that I want to lay stress.

Renewal in Worship

Throughout this report the word 'Christianise' is used as in many cases this is as far as we have got. Worship tends to be stagnant and there is a great resistance to any change. However, in areas in which there has been effective evangelism and church-planting, we are beginning to see a new vitality entering into worship, along with the introduction of indigenous rather than imported factors. This new vitality of worship could on occasions be designated 'charismatic', but this is by no means always the case. However, there is also a deepening of personal commitment and a greater readiness to proclaim the Gospel publicly. There is sometimes resistance from the more conservative element, but that seems to be a fairly common condition world-wide.

This renewal of worship seems in almost every congregation in which it has taken place, to be initiated by the women, and to leave the young people only marginally touched. This is a deep concern, bearing in mind that large numbers of young people have difficulty in seeing how even the renewed worship relates at all to the situation, political and otherwise, in the world. They find difficulty in identifying the needs and interests of their generation with it.

With worship goes witness. We are able to discern definite changes in personal attitudes and behaviour, in relationships, and in social patterns in certain sections of the community. Witness does not only means the actual sharing of the Gospel with others, though this takes place where we see evangelism deepening, but it also results in changed lifestyles in homes. Once again, this is less marked amongst the younger generation.

Giving
There seems to be a direct relationship between the effectiveness of evangelistic activity and the giving of individuals in a congregation. This indicator usually drags its heels in the rear. But wherever there has been a new sense of outreach and evangelism, giving has increased particularly among the professional classes. There is a greater tendency to give generously amongst the second generation professional people than the first.

Young People
In all these areas, the indicators tend to show a reluctance and a resistance amongst young people. And yet most of the congregations are packed with young people. It is not as though they have left the Church because they feel it is not meeting their needs. They are all there, but they seem to respond more slowly to the presentation of the Gospel and to the conforming of their lives to the claims of Jesus. We are giving a great deal of attention to this. Do they come to church merely because there is nothing much else to do in rural areas? Or is there a genuine battle going on within them in terms of spiritual loyalties? The Diocese is giving more and more time to the development of youth groups in both the towns and the rural areas. We are beginning to be able to analyse more accurately what exactly is going on in the young mind. Inevitably, and particularly in the South African situation, there appears to be a high degree of confusion and frustration.

Methods

The Diocese is less than three years old and I have been in it for only two years. So it would be premature to talk of effective methods. We are at a stage of analysis and experimentation, particularly as this area has been so neglected in the past. We have inherited a conventional Anglican parish system. But these are not parishes in the urban or British sense of the word. A parish consists of a vast tract of territory with one main church at a central point and anything up to forty chapelries or congregations dotted all over it. These impossible parishes are staffed by one or two priests, who have to spend a great deal of their time rushing round celebrating the sacraments or taking services. No wonder growth has been so slow. We have no money and are woefully under-staffed.

However, we have tried to take a long, hard look at our situation and to wait upon the Lord as to the way forward in effective evangelism and church-planting. We have also made a policy decision that we will not seek for financial help from outside the Diocese. In its present situation, the Diocese can never be rich. But we believe that there are sufficient human and material resources within it to do the work that God has brought it into existence to do.

Training

We lay much emphasis on lay-training. A great deal of the service-taking and pastoral work, both in the rural and urban areas, can be done by suitably trained lay persons. We are, therefore, in the process of training worship leaders, evangelists, healers, pastoral workers, youth workers and administrators. We are also seeking to create a large number of competent disciplers. This all sounds very grand, but I need to emphasize that it is the vision towards which we are moving, and that we are only in the rudimentary stages.

In the process of training, we are already discovering ordinary men in every situation who, knowing and loving the Lord, are competent for training as self-supporting priests (or local priests). A very important factor in whether a man should be ordained to the priesthood is whether he has the respect and support of the local community. The fact that there is an ordained leader in local congregations, who is able to celebrate the sacraments, takes a great deal of weight off the shoulders of the stipendiary clergy. It is also leading us to reconsider the requirements of men who offer themselves for the stipendiary ministry.

In a Diocese which has little money for the training of full-time priests, we feel that we have to make sure that we are stewarding our resources responsibly. We are, therefore, insisting more and more on the necessity of men having clear teaching gifts before they can go forward for training for the stipendiary ministry (at the time of writing, women may not be ordained to the priesthood in this province). The pattern which we are seeking to produce is one of a small number of stipendiary clergy, who can be supported financially adequately by the Diocese. They have been trained in the teaching gifts they already possess. They move around and give ongoing training to the increasing number of self-supporting or local clergy who are to be dotted around the Diocese. A great deal of emphasis will be given to evangelism, discipling and church-planting in this training.

We are specifically looking for training colleges for our stipendiary clergy which have a strong outreach and mission emphasis. We believe that a great deal of the theological training which has been given to ordinands in the past is not really relevant to the needs of a predominantly outreach diocese. We are also seeking to train persons with the gift of evangelism to evangelize in their own particular areas. In one or two places, we have started taking full-time evangelists onto the Diocesan payroll in order that they may create a model for others to follow.

A number of the key evangelists whom we have discovered in the Diocese are young people. This is most encouraging in view of some of the discouragements mentioned above. We believe that once the Holy Spirit gets amongst the young people, we may well see something quite revolutionary taking place in the Diocese. However, evangelism to the young people must be set very clearly within the context of the political and social developments of South Africa. An evangelism which is isolated from the real world in which most of the young people are growing up and living, will merely attract spiritual drop-outs and isolate the bulk of the young people even more from both the proclamation of the Gospel and from the Church. We are giving a great deal of attention to relating evangelism and disciplining to context.

Message

Apart from the conventional A.B.C.D. of the Gospel, we have found it necessary to emphasize certain aspects of the message.

Many people in this area have at some time past been subject to what is clearly a very sacramental theology. Consequently for many churchgoers salvation has been seen to be by baptism and confirmation. It has been difficult to persuade people that this is not the case. It is very difficult to convince people of their need of salvation when they are convinced that, because of their participation in the sacraments and other rites, they are already saved. There is a very natural human resistance to any teaching which may cast doubt upon this. We have tried to teach in such a way as to put the sacraments in their correct perspective, and to call people to personal repentance and faith.

Assurance
The doctrine of assurance has also been almost totally unknown in the Diocese. Consequently much genuine Christian faith and witness has been weakened. We are therefore spending quite a lot of time in our teaching in the churches leading people to an understanding of what God has promised us in Jesus Christ, and of the total reliability of the promises of God. To many, this is totally new. While some receive it with joy and thanksgiving, others find it difficult to absorb into their own theological mindset. However, whenever people have begun to understand the promises of God, we have found a newness of life and a more confident witness.

Healing
Traditional beliefs, the syncretistic bodies, particularly the Z.C.C., and other more orthodox bodies lay a great deal of stress on spirits and healing. Many people come to a hearing of the Gospel out of this particular background. We are, therefore, laying great stress on Jesus as the one who has conquered everything in the spiritual realm, and who is able to heal. The clergy and I together have been doing a lot of study in the whole area of healing. A great deal of healing is now taking place in the ministry of the Gospel through people throughout the Diocese. The power of the Kingdom must be seen visibly in our preaching, and we are giving this a great deal of attention.

The Political and Economic Dimension
In dealing with young people, evangelism cannot be divorced from the whole political situation. Jesus made it clear that the cost had to be counted before commitment was made. Although that cost spreads through many aspects of human life, in South

Africa it is very prominent in the whole area of political loyalty and commitment. Being a Christian means that there are certain things that one cannot do. Where young people are being told that they are sell-outs if they do not involve themselves in violence or who believe that if they are Christians they can play no part whatever in the liberation struggle, this issue of cost has to be made very clear. To be in Christ will involve them in the liberation struggle and will prevent their being involved in violence. This puts them clearly in the cross-fire, and they must know it before they commit themselves. They must know that commitment to Jesus requires an obedience which has both positive and negative aspects in the political and economic context. Not to say all this makes evangelism both irrelevant to the situation and untrue to the model that Jesus himself gave us.

I am thinking primarily of black young people. There are very few white Anglican young people in this Diocese because there are so very few English-speaking primary and secondary schools. Consequently, most Anglican young people are sent to school in the big cities outside the Diocese. Nevertheless, even in the evangelizing of white young people, the whole issue of involvement in the liberation struggle, and just how that involvement is to be played out, must be made clear in the presentation of the Gospel. We have had too much of people, young and old, claiming that they have "accepted Christ as their Lord and Saviour" who, when presented with the political and economic responsibilities of Christian discipleship, will claim that that was not "part of the package". It must be made very clear that the "package" of Christian discipleship is the totality of life.

The evangelistic message in the context of rural traditionalism must include the ministry of the Holy Spirit. In a mindset in which the spiritual world is such a reality and in which spirits play so large a part, the person and work of the Holy Spirit must be given a great deal of emphasis in the actual preaching of the Gospel as well as in the discipling which follows.

Resistance

The most powerful resistance to the presentation of the Gospel at the moment comes from those who have been brought up in a different theology, and who believe that it is through baptism and confirmation that salvation is achieved. It is not difficult to understand why people who all their lives have thought that they were "okay" should suddenly have that assurance questioned. In various places there is outright opposition to clergy and lay-leadership in the parishes. I am asked to have such persons removed because what they are proclaiming is "unanglican." Most resistance comes from the bureaucratic and professional classes, while the ordinary people are only too happy to respond to the claims of Jesus.

The racial implications of the Gospel are also being strongly resisted in some of the white communities. While many white communities are growing in their realization of our oneness in Christ, and are taking action to make this a practical reality, in others so-called "converted" people are leaving because black faces are appearing in congregations. There is a real fear that the ethos of services will be changed. This resistance shows itself in people voting with their feet, and going elsewhere.

Chapter Nine

India: Evangelism among the urban poor

Vinay Samuel

A description of Divya Shanthi Association and Trust's Ministry in New Lingarajapuram Slum Dwellers Resettlement Area, Bangalore.

Introduction

On September 13, 1987 about 2300 families were moved from their residence of 14 years in a slum on the dried up Millers Tank bed in the heart of the city of Bangalore. They were moved between 7.00 p.m. and 3.00 a.m. and literally dumped on a casually prepared site of fifty acres in the Lingarajapuram area. Each family was given a plot of 15ft by 20ft, five sheets of asbestos, each sheet measuring 8ft by 4ft and Rs.30/- (approximately US $2.00 at that time) to start a new life.

Four borewells with handpumps were provided and two temporary toilet blocks with 12 cubicles each. This was in some ways an improvement from their situation in Miller's Tank where 2300 families lived on a four acre plot of land with no water or toilet facilities.

Entry Point

Divya Shanthi Christian Association and Trust has worked in Lingarajapuram since 1978. The beginnings of the work go back to 1967 when Colleen Philipsz (later Colleen Samuel) soon after her conversion to Christ began a children's club under the shade of a large tree in an area known for its poverty and lack of every conceivable civic amenity.[1]

The Association and Trust's ministries focused on education, health care, vocational training, adult education, community organization and sharing the Good News.

The Association and Trust responded two days after the Millers Tank slum dwellers were shifted. They found a most unfortunate situation. Heavy rains meant that the people could not put up even adequate temporary shelters. Having been moved 5 kilometres, most of those who worked as domestic workers lost their jobs. Children could not attend school. Nearly 60% of the adults were self-employed as street vendors. Their working capital disappeared in the three days they could not work. Cholera reared its head. In the first week, four children died each day.

A team was put together and their response to the situation was to provide immediate relief. Liaising with state authorities, the Christian team facilitated in the provision of street lights, more borewells and toilets, better roads, sanitation and drainage. Bus facilities with free passes for the school children were provided. Working with service clubs like the Rotary, immunization, health camps etc. were provided. A revolving credit programme was launched immediately and nearly 500 families were provided with working capital (average Rs 300/- = £15) to restart their micro-business activities. Some children were found places in local schools. With the assistance of an evangelical relief and development agency, more housing material was provided to make temporary shelter habitable. The entry point focused on advocacy for the people with state authorities and emergency relief.

Places of Worship

From the beginning, the team worked with the local leaders. The people said that their most important need was for places of worship, temples, a mosque and a church. The team assisted in getting land allocated for them. The people accepted that we gave priority to religious needs and that we respected their religious sentiments.

In the first three weeks an incident took place which taught us a great deal. The state was keen on demolishing a mosque on the Millers Tank bed before handing over the land to developers. They were apprehensive about possible communal problems. Fundamentalist Islamic groups took it up as an issue. The papers joined in, and the situation was rapidly getting out of control.

Colleen and the team met the Chief Minister of the State and other officials. They visited the resettlement area and handed over the site for a mosque to the local mosque committee. They also promised assistance for the construction of a mosque. Colleen also invited three wealthy Muslim businessmen to be present, who donated the necessary finance for the building. All this was in public at a typically Indian function in a very festive atmosphere.

The next day, the state authorities demolished the mosque and no protest was heard. It also resulted in building very cordial relationships with the Muslims who constitute almost 50% of the resettlement community.

Continuing Ministry

The State provided land to the Association for its work. Temporary structures were put up. A school was started. A medical programme with six health workers from the community was launched. A clinic with a doctor and nurses started functioning. The major thust was in the adult education programme with 12 adult educators, most of whom were from the community. In all 800 adults participate in the programme. The Bible is used as the basis. The trainees meet three times a week with the co-ordinator to prepare lessons and debrief. Most adult education groups have a regular prayer and Bible study cell attached to them. 48 groups function in the area. Vocational training for young people was launched in producing leather products, fibre-glass products, handicrafts, garments and in the engineering unit. The revolving credit programme grew rapidly to cover over 300 participants at any given time. A new programme forms smaller credit groups which save and lend and run their programmes themselves. Our staff provide technical assistance.

Two senior evangelists, one male and the other female, are part of the team. They train the community workers, adult education workers, and health workers in ways of sharing the Gospel through their work. They themselves organise prayer meetings, worship activities and evangelistic events. The evangelistic events are organised during festival times and fit equally into the pattern of community life.

The Gospel is constantly shared in the way the activities are run. Each group/unit/team spends time in prayer and worship daily. Each community worker visits at least 25 families each during the day. Some of their time is always spent in counselling and prayer. All community workers go through a training period every week.

A major area of work is with the police. The police send battered and abandoned wives, abandoned children and families without shelter to us regularly. We are asked to assist in defusing tension between groups in the community. Our close work with the police has not alienated us from the community. On the contrary, both the community and the police see us as a bridge between the two. Colleen is now a Special Police Officer for the area. Counselling people sent by the police and others who come on their own is taking up a significant portion of our time but is very rewarding spiritually.

We are also openly involved in the political concerns of our community as they are critical for the well being of the people. We seek to make the people aware of political realities and alternatives.

Evangelistic Impact

Due to the public nature of our work, especially with our open involvement in the political concerns of the community, we are objects of constant scrutiny by political parties and the state intelligence departments. We allow them access to all our records and activities. We have therefore not baptized anyone from a non-Christian faith from the resettlement community. To date more than a score have taken baptism on their own with local pentecostal groups that have sprung up in the community.

They continue to be nurtured through our daily worship times and our regular bible studies and retreats. About 30 adults from the community work in the programme. Twenty of them come from Muslim or Hindu backgrounds. All of them now worship Christ alone. They are regular at daily worship and articulate in prayer.

Out of the eight hundred people in the adult education programmes, more than 90% come from Muslim and Hindu backgrounds. At least 50% of those would say that Christ has become real to them in the past two years.

Problems

We have begun an in-depth evaluation of the evangelistic impact of our work using a variety of instruments of evaluation.

Many of the people who worship Christ continue to have a religious life mixed with a variety of superstitions and old beliefs. When they pray they sound deeply spiritual and even mature. Such spirituality is often absent in the way they relate to work, money, and neighbours.

Once a church is planted, the pressure of nurturing a church requires much energy. This introduces conflict between the pressure to maintain the upbuilding of the congregation and other areas of witness and mission. Making Christ known, enabling individuals to come to Christ does not introduce the same tensions as enabling a local worshipping community to become Christian disciples. The discipling ministry now demands a lot of energy. With limited resources can energy and resources be diverted to that end?

The harvest is ready. We face no major obstacles to sharing the Gospel. The people are eager to hear. Many believe too easily. We are not sure how far we should go in planting churches and nurturing those who come to Christ. If the decision is left to the community, they prefer independent churches on the pentecostal model.

Reaching a People

After 15 years of intensive ministry among the poor in the area, the following perspectives have emerged about reaching a people group.

1. A people group is a community which has socio-economic dimensions to its identity apart from the obviously cultural, religious and ethnic factors.
2. Among the urban poor, a community is hard to define. Socio-economic and religious factors are the most dominant. Religious differences are not sharp as popular religion underlies religious belief and practice.

3. Evangelism happens and Christian faith takes root when -
   (a) a worshipping community is established made up mostly of local resident believers.
   (b) They are accepted as a legitimate religious group in the community.
   (c) Their worship is culturally appropriate.
   (d) Commitment to sharing the Gospel with the rest of the community becomes a dominant force in their Christian life.
   (e) As a church, they are not inward looking, struggling to gain acceptance and security in the communities, but confident of their place in the community, and desirous of reaching out in evangelism and service to others.
   (f) Their evangelistic activities are patronised by the community. Other religious leaders tolerate their presence and activity.
   (g) Conversions and baptism take place regularly as a normal outcome of Gospel sharing activities.
   (h) The church's concern for the total needs of the community is recognized and affirmed by other sections of the community.
   (i) The church contributes its share of community leaders.

4. In a religiously plural context like ours, we think it is not viable to define a people group as reached quantitively, for example when 20% of the people are converted and baptized. It is also not adequate to plant a Christian presence among a people group. The relationship of the Christian presence to the rest of the community, its acceptance by the community, and the evangelistic activities it carries out help define how far a people group/community is reached.

5. Our goal for the resettlement area is to reach the community there through the establishment of a church in each of the three residential segments of the area.

Footnotes

1. See further "From Privilege to Poverty" in *Lifestyle in the Eighties* Edited by Ron Sider (Exeter, Paternoster Press 1982).

Chapter Ten

Women's role in Evangelism

Juliet Thomas

Context

India is a land of tremendous contrasts – of rich beauty of incredible filth, of extravagant wealth and incredible poverty, of wondrous architecture and lowly mud tenements. We are 850 million people of whom only 2.8% are Christian. We have about 756 dialects, and 200 written languages. In our 22 states our cultures and customs are widely varied. We are diverse and divided. In some of our states conversion is banned. There are 600,000 villages, many of which have still not been reached with the Gospel of Jesus Christ.

Religious thinking and teaching often shape one's values and one's worth. A traditional Hindu would believe that a person cannot attain salvation as a woman except through being reborn as a man. This is her Karma. They would also believe that a woman is irresponsible: so in childhood she obeys her father, in youth she obeys her husband and in old age she obeys her son.

In the Koran "Men have authority over women because Allah has made the one superior to the other . . . As for those from whom you fear disobedience, admonish them . . . beat them".

Christianity teaches that a woman, like a man, is created in the image of God. She is redeemed in Christ to be "joint-heir of the grace of life". There is no male or female before God.

Someone has graphically described the plight of women in our society thus:

Woman bent over by the weight of the world
   — family . . . . society . . . . Church
never allowed to stand straight.

Bent over by loads of bricks
   — of stone . . . of water. . . of baskets of wares.

Bending over the fireplace
— the washing stone . . . the ironing board . . .
  the grinding stone.

Bent over by
— racism . . . caste . . . religion . . . and class.

Bent over by unjust structures
— social . . . political . . . economic . . . cultural
never allowed to stand straight.

Woman bent over under the fury of
— a husband's rage . . . a capitalist's greed
— a landlord's lust . . . a cruel world's dictate.

Woman is
— not meant to . . . not supposed to
— not allowed to stand straight.

Woman broken inside
Spiritually abused and diseased
derided, bullied, beaten even burnt to death!
depressed, miserable, thinking nothing of herself,
believing that her destiny is her bent-over state.

History

In the 19th century the Church pioneered the education of women. They were trained as doctors and nurses to treat other women. Though the Church pioneered these reforms in society, it has never fully opened its own doors to women in the years of "Mission" before independence in 1947. Jane Hatfield's research revealed the following:

* Women missionaries who were competent and financially independent were not replaced by Indian women, because women's ministry was not held in high respect. So parents discouraged their daughters from entering a career which would make them a less desirable match in marriage. Furthermore, the churches prefer to train men whom congregations would readily accept.

* The churches became preoccupied trying to establish their position in the Indian society after the colonial rule. Women's work was thus relegated often to avoid antagonism.[1]

The encouragement of women in ministry still faces similar struggles today. We cannot talk of 'evangelising' women till the Christian women are themselves built up to understand their role and be aware of their responsibilities.

In 1982, I co-ordinated the work among women under the Bangalore Penetration Plan. Though I had been in Bangalore since 1962, I had never been aware of the needs of women. For the first time I walked into a slum, half a kilometre from home. I was shocked at what I saw. Since then the Spirit of God has been compelling me into working among women. I was a teacher and happy in my work and ministry among students. For one long year I struggled. Evelyn Christenson whose Prayer Seminars I co-ordinated in India, put her hand on my shoulder and commissioned me to women's work. I was staggered but yielded to God's will.

Because of our culture it is very difficult in leadership positions in evangelical circles. For most of us it is a lonely struggle. Recognising God has called me into Indian Women's ministry, Operation Mobilisation offered their umbrella under which I have been working since 1988. I value greatly the strong prayer base and warm encouragement from brothers and sisters of the O.M. family both in India and overseas.

I dream to see Indian woman free from her shackles and chains, to see her blossom forth in beauty and maturity for which she has been created. I labour and toil to this end.

Message

The Manila Manifesto states that "God created men and women as equal bearers of his image (Gen. 1:26–27), accepts them equally in Christ (Gal. 3:28) and poured out his Spirit on all flesh, sons and daughters alike (Acts 2:17–18). In addition, because the Holy Spirit distributes his gifts to women as well as to men, they must be given opportunities to exercise their gifts. We celebrate their distinguished record in the history of missions and are convinced that God calls women to similar roles today.

Even though we are not fully agreed what forms their leadership should take, we do agree about the partnership in world evangelization which God intends men and women to enjoy. Suitable training must therefore be made available to both."[2]

John Stott affirms:
"There is a general presumption in favour of women in ministry (including leadership and teaching). It is that on the Day of Pentecost, in fulfilment of prophecy, God poured out his Spirit on 'all flesh', including 'sons and daughters' and his servants, both men and women. If the gift of the Spirit was bestowed on all believers of both sexes, so were his gifts. There is no evidence, or even hint, that the charismata were restricted to men. On the contrary, the Spirit's gifts were distributed to all for the common good, making possible what is often called as 'every member ministry of the Body of Christ'. We must conclude, therefore, not only that Christ gives charismata (including the teaching gifts) to women, but that alongside his gifts he issues his call to develop and exercise them in his service and in the service of others for the building up of his body."[3]

The Lord is building his Church. But how can he build, "how can the Church rise while the gifts of three-fourths of her membership are sepulchred in her midst?"
"Daughters of Zion, from the dust
Exalt thy fallen head;
Again in thy Redeemer trust
He calls thee from the dead."

Resistance

Our Culture and Society
Women have a low place in our society and are treated more as chattels to be used and exploited rather then persons to be loved and developed.

According traditional Hindu teaching, the ideal wife took Rama's, wife, Sita, famous for her subjugation of her individuality, as her model. Such a perfect wife regarded her husband as her god and obeyed him even if he lacked good qualities, was diseased or an alcoholic. This was her dharma (duty) and the means of her salvation.

The status of the Indian women has gone through a continuous process of change. But through it all runs the dominating thread of her 'low self-image' imposed upon her by family, Church and society from the time of her birth till her death.

At Birth
Boys are preferred to girls. In 1986 a report that appeared in 'India Today' about the practice of killing girl babies that is still prevalent in some communities and is becoming increasingly widespread today. A girl is a liability.

At Marriage
Tradition clothes the husband with a 'god-image'. In many places, new brides prostrate themselves at their husband's feet on the threshold of her new home. This symbolises her servitude to him all her life. No matter how she is treated in her husband's home normally she can no longer go back to her parents.

One Indian proverb says "Woman is like spit; once spat out she cannot be taken back."

One magazine described women as 'the poorest of the poor, oppressed of the oppressed'. One Christian leader maintained that 'the largest untouched people-group in India is women'.

Due to this oppression, exploitation and suppression the Joint Women's Organizations have begun to voice their angry and violent protest against these injustices and inequalities. Only the feminist activist's voice is heard. Though these Joint Women's Organizations have done laudable work, they have in the process pitted woman against her God and man. For all purposes the Indian female evangelical voice is almost non-existent in the society. Women need to hear in loud and clear tones and know that they can reach their full potential in Christ.

Self-oppression of Women themselves
Woman's low self-image gives her a deep sense of inadequacy and helplessness. She is full of fear and is a victim of prejudices. She is a silent sufferer.

Vicky is a young woman who shares her struggles and longings:

"True 'untold millions are still untold, untold millions are outside the fold'. 'Lord I'm aware of your concern for mankind here am I, but send my brother'.

"I love the Lord and so want to please him. But I'm only a girl and I can't even look at a little lizard, leave alone a snake! How can I go far away, in heathen darkness dwelling, to tell the millions who for ever may be lost unless someone tells them salvation's story.

"A common excuse many women tend to make is 'No one would listen to us women in this land. It is our culture.' Some say that women are meant for the kitchen only. No one will believe or accept what a woman says. And yet .. did not God use many women even in our country to fulfil his purposes? Will not this challenge us to go? All we need is to obey and trust the Lord to enable us.

"I needed to move on . . . to a village known for its low moral living. The people spoke a strange language and their way of living was some times shocking and depressing. God had opened a wide door for effective ministry. Would I trust God and obey in spite of all the fears welling within me? Again the excuse of my womanhood stood strongly before me. 'It's a risk Lord'. Even the local people in the district said so. 'Act like men, be strong' (I Cor 16:9,13)"

Church

The Manila Manifesto states that "we deeply regret that many of our congregations are inward-looking, organized for maintenance rather than mission, or preoccupied with church-based activities at the expense of witness".

It is profoundly disturbing to face the possibility that over a long period of time the Church may have been denying to women the place assigned to them by God. But there is no growth with pain and struggle and in this area as in others, the Church must come to maturity.

It is true : "The Church is God's agent in the earth – the medium through which he expresses himself to the World." Could we then seriously ask ourselves whether the reason God has not been able to *fully* express himself to the world, the reason the Church is not marching forward in Christ's mission in the world, is because she is not a fully functioning Church? She is handicapped and crippled particularly because the tremendous potential and possibilites of women have not been developed.

Effect

Women need to be assured again of their identity in Christ. Inspite of their cultural inhibitions and natural timidity, they need to be taught and trained to take up their responsibilities and encouraged to develop their God-given gifts for the building up of the family, the church and in the extension of his Kingdom. This is what under O.M., I have been seeking to do across the country through Conferences, Family Life Seminars, Prayer Seminars, Training Programmes and through different Workshops. In many places I find that this is a new emphasis and message for them. They are excited, totally open and show deep hunger for the things of God.

Through these ministries, women's leadership has been developed, families are reconciled and enriched, women's gifts for service are released and developed and slum women are being reached.

This year I am trying to network women for the purpose of encouraging and spurring one another to good works. I'm also seeking to develop ministries among women such as prayer, bible study and slum ministry. I am trying this in Bangalore. I believe every Christian woman needs to be involved in these three areas. I am also trying to provide materials for teaching / training purposes written by Indian women in our context to meet our particular needs.

I sense a new awakening among women. It is exciting as it were, 'to see them emerging from their cocoons'. Social activism left in its wake an emptiness creating within a deep need for a deeper experience of God and hunger for his Word. A spirit of prayer has gripped our people. God is moving in pockets of people here and there. We have passed from despair and hopelessness to yearning and longing. I believe we are now entering yet another phase – that of expectation. And who can indeed estimate what God can do through women whose hearts are burdened for a broken world, filled with God's love and empowered by the Holy Spirit to communicate the love of Christ?

Methods

Women Reaching Women for Effective Evangelism
1. Special Centres of Studies and Training for Women

Feminine perspectives, insights and understanding of women's needs in family and society.

2. *Individual gifts*
These should be harnessed and strengthened and women should be released to develop special women's ministries, for example among servants, the mentally disturbed, the aged, prisoners, prostitutes and women in slums; and in sick visiting, hospitality (an open home etc.), prayer, counselling and Bible study.

3. *Church*
as the base for mobilising women.

a) Recognition : The God given gifts, talents, and abilities of women should be recognized by the Church, so that the women can be involved in various aspects of the ministry to a much greater measure than occurs at present.

b) Teaching and Training : Adequate teaching materials on the biblical teaching on women should be provided by compiling existing materials and writing additional materials.

c) Encouragement to Serve : The local churches should motivate and encourage Christian women to work chiefly among Hindu women in a holistic ministry using bridges like the following: Christian festivals, sewing and cooking classes, adult literacy classes, hospital visitation, neighbourhood children's work, neighbourhood Bible studies. Rejected and neglected groups, such as prostitutes and prisoners, should be a special focus for evangelism.

4. *Christian Homes*
These can become centres of caring and nurture of new converts and rehabilitated persons.

When young Hindu women become Christians, they often receive no nurture. Hence they easily slip back into the religious and cultural customs of their homes. Christian homes in their own community should be sought out for the purpose of spiritual nurture and establishment, including marriage arrangements if necessary. [4]

5. *Ministry of Friendship*
The ministry of friendship means infinite expenditure of time, sympathy and love to place ourselves alongside these women to

enter into their lives, to share their aspirations in so far as these are right; it means willingness also to lay ourselves open to not a few snubs and repulses. In many ways it is harder than contact with the poorer classes, who often quickly and gratefully respond, and do not so speedily pull us up by their hot resentment the instant we show the cloven hoof of our fancied superiority and behave as if we had come to "work among them" rather than to love them and seek their friendship.

A young medical doctor felt led to open a clinic in a predominantly Muslim area with the help of her husband. Very soon she found the Muslim women coming to her in large numbers. What was the reason? Was it because they could not go to men doctors? That was of course an important reason. But there was another. Word spread around that this lady doctor listened to them as they poured out their hearts to her. She loved them and expressed her understanding and concern for them. So they came. In many cultures today only women can reach women.

6. *Men and Women Co-ordinated*
Men's and women's work should be closely co-ordinated, so that whenever a woman is under instruction, one of the men missionaries can be relating to her husband, and vice versa; so that whole families may be won for Christ and wherever possible the terrible divisions and break up of homes may be averted. At present in India we not infrequently see whole districts in which there are only women missionaries and other districts in which only men are working, and the result is a terrible hindering of the progress of the Gospel.

7. *Literature*
One of the great lines of cleavage lies in the women-hearts of Hinduism; it is the women who are moulding its baby sons and daughters in myriads today; it is the influence of wife and mother that holds back many a secret convert from confession; it is the women who can be a powerful factor in the upheaval to liberty when it comes. How could these women be reached? There is an ever increasing body of women who can read and who can be influenced in their homes beyond all telling, if only we had the right literature to give them.

8. *Culture*

In India which is predominantly Hindu, the mother's influence over the children, both boys and girls, up to about ten years of age, is paramount, and women are the conservative element in the defence of their faith. We ought to lay far more emphasis on work among Hindu women as a means for hastening the evangelism for Indians. There needs to be an understanding of the customs and culture that rule their behaviour and thinking patterns. Only then can the Gospel be made relevant to them.

9. *Caste*

One of the greatest cultural barriers to the Gospel in modern history has been the caste system – a powerful institution in India that has frustrated the work of missionaries for centuries. Much of India is still deeply enmeshed in the caste system. How to approach the caste system, therefore, continues to be a knotty issue. One of the most significant missiological studies to appear on the subject in recent years has come from the pen of B.V. Subbamma, a caste-hindu whose own pilgrimage to Christianity was hindered by caste.

Subbamma was introduced to Christianity as a child while attending a Lutheran mission school in South India. She initially resisted biblical teachings, believing Christianity was religion of the Harijans (outcasts). Eventually however, after reading the Bible for herself, her life was transformed: "The name of Jesus became so precious to me that I could hardly believe it . . . I was supremely happy, having the assurance that Jesus Christ had suffered for my sin and had forgiven me and blessed me with salvation." A major obstacle, however loomed before her: "The question of baptism disturbed me. I was definitely not prepared to leave my own Kamma people and join some other community. At the same time I longed to be baptized since I understood one had to be baptized if she wished to be a disciple of the Lord." After enduring considerable personal turmoil and opposition from her family, Subbamma was baptized and paid the tremendous price of complete identification with the existing Church made up of Harijan Christians.

10. *The Outcast*

The poor and illiterate are often the untouched amongst whom even Christian women are reluctant to minister. Women in

Bombay spend Rs. 100 a day on a slimming clinic whereas the
Adivasi women in Orissa would sell their babies for Rs. 100 in
order to survive.

On the average 70% of the women are illiterate, about 65%
under-nourished, and 45% live below the poverty level. Women
must be involved in meeting these needs through adult literacy
classes, income generating schemes, and employment skills.

Prostitutes carry a social stigma. Fear of this rubbing on to
them prevents many Christians from having anything to do with
them and to help them.

Dr. I S Gilada, the Honorary President of the Indian Health
Organization, reported that there are more than 300,000
prostitutes in the metropolitan cities of Bombay, Delhi, Calcutta,
Pune and Nagpur. Poverty and unemployment are some of the
causes for this.

It has been reported that 25% of the women in the red light
areas of Bombay have been abducted and sold; 8% have been
sold by their fathers after they had been forced into incenstuous
relationships. Nearly 6% were raped and sold later while 15%
had been dedicated to the Goddess Yellamma. The Yellamma
system in Karnataka alone anually sends around 8,000 girls to
the brothels in Pune and Bombay. Almost 150,000 prostitutes in
Bombay and Pune constitute the single largest profession for
working women in the city. In Pune 15 to 20% of the women
were sold to prostitution by their husbands. Morally they have
lost everything – even their own self-respect.

However good a Government rehabilitation programme may
be for these prostitutes, who have been removed from the
brothels and brought into Rehabilitation Centres, they still feel
degraded and unclean. Only Christ can offer forgiveness and
cleansing so that they can be transformed into new persons to
start life afresh.

Prayer
Pray that with undaunting courage, spurred by confidence in our
God and our intense love for our people, we Christian women
will help to set aside prejudices, break down barriers, and rise
above pressures in order that we may go forth to touch others for
Christ. Lord restore unto us our sense of worth, the dignity of
our womanhood.

Pray that God may raise many women in my land who would, like Esther, be willing to be instruments of purpose in God's hands – cleansed and available for use – who with her would say 'And if I perish, I perish!'

Questions for discussion

Training
Q. Why do men get preference over women?
Is there a need for special training for women giving feminine perspectives and understanding of women's needs? Is there a need for short courses for women only.

Structures
Q. What can be done about the problem of power and control in a hierarchical church structure which keeps women at a lower range and prevents them from developing their gifts?

Footnotes

1. From research done by Dss. Jane Hatfield in a study done at United Theological College, Bangalore.
2. *The Manila Manifesto* published by The Lausanne Committee for World Evangelisation was produced at the Lausanne II Congress on World Evangelisation, manila, July 1989. It is published by LCWE, 2531 Nina Street, Pasadena, California, USA.
3. John Stott in *Issues Facing Christians Today* (Basingstoke, Marshalls).
4. From Lausanne Occasional Papers on "Reaching Hindus".

Chapter Eleven

Brazil: Evangelism in a Missionary Diocese

Robinson Cavalcanti

This paper aims to describe and analyse the Anglican Evangelistic action in the North East Region of Brazil, South America between 1975 and 1990.

The Country

Brazil is the largest and most populous country of Latin America, colonized by the Portuguese since 1500, independent as a constitutional monarchy since 1882 , and a Federal Republic since 1889. Its population is about 140 million, the majority of whom are a mixture of Portuguese, African and natives. The national language is Portuguese.

Religion

Over 80% of the population consider themselves Roman Catholic. Out of those only 10% attend a Church regularly. 50% of the Roman Catholics are in some way connected or influenced by the occult. The majority of the population live a nominal Christian life and only go to church for baptisms, weddings and funerals.

About 8% of the population is Protestant and two-thirds of them are Pentecostal. The others are from immigrants (such as Lutherans) or from North American Missions (like the Baptists, Presbyterians and Methodists).

Missionary Protestantism arrived in the mid 19th century with an ideology of modernization, appealing to the emerging middle class with their good high schools. Pentecostalism arrived in 1910 working mainly with the poor.

The Anglicans

Anglicans have been present in Brazil since Independence with consular chapels and also, years later, with some Japanese immigrants. A North American Episcopal Mission was established in the extreme south in 1890. Today the Episcopal Church of Brazil is an autonomous Province in the Anglican Communion, with 7 dioceses and about 150 parishes and missions.

During the first 50 years the Episcopal (Anglican) Church had an evangelical and evangelistic character, and grew very fast. After the Second World War the Church suffered from the strong influence of liberal-catholic thought, losing its impulse, with a crisis of identity and a decline in membership in the 1960's and 1970's. The Church lost part of its clergy when it became an autonomous Province and stopped receiving salaries from the U.S.A.

The last 15 years have shown a slow evangelical recovery and a charismatic presence, which some of the hierarchy still strongly discriminate against and repress. The younger clergy tend to opt for Liberation Theology.

The Region

North East Brazil is the oldest part of the country and where one third of the population live. At the same time, it is the most impoverished with only one third of the national per capita income. The majority of the population lives in the rural area, oppressed by landlords and the traditional families. In the big cities there are many slums, unemployment, abandoned children, illiteracy and violence. The poor tend to follow the occult, folk Roman-Catholicism or Pentecostalism. After Vatican II the region received the influence of Liberation Theology with the formation of the Base Ecclesial Communities. Today we see a conservative reconquest in the Roman Catholic Church under John Paul II.

Anglican Evangelisation

In 1975, the Church Synod responded to a proposal of the North American missionary Bishop Edmund Knox Sherrill, and decided to inaugurate a project to create a Missionary Anglican Diocese in North East Brazil. The aim was to transform the ancient British consular chapels in national middle-class parishes and to create new missions among the poor. The pilot project would be the parish of Holy Trinity in the city of Recife (1,200.000 inhabitants) under the responsibility of the Rev. Paulo Ruiz Garcia, an evangelical orientated minister from Sao Paulo. At the same time some South American Missionary Society (SAMS) missionaries were invited to join the pioneer team.

Bishop Sherrill who was living in Rio de Janeiro at the time, moved to Recife. He sought to lead the new diocese, train new workers, and look for cooperation with evangelical denominations.

The first group to join the Church were Protestants escaping from extreme fundamentalist, legalist, separatist and politically conservative communities. A second group came from the Roman Catholic Church escaping nominalism and non-biblical doctrines or the horizontalism of Liberation Theology.

Staff workers from other evangelical denominations were employed to help in the administration and in Christian education. Our theological students attended their seminaries with complementary Anglican education by the Bishop.

South American Missionary Society missionaries were responsible for the opening of four new missions and the young Brazilians for two others.

Methodology

For the Middle-class Communities
1. Propagation by mass media of Anglicanism and its activities in the Region.

2. The main evangelistic strategy has centred on The "Encounter" Movement including Marriage Encounter, Youth Encounter, Teenager's Encounter and Children's Encounter with Christ. This method originated from the Roman Catholic Church, but was adapted for use evangelistically.

3. The "Cursillo" Movement was also borrowed from Roman Catholic practice. The "Cursillo" movement was founded in

1948. People were invited to week-end retreats covering basic doctrines in separate sex groupings to avoid the issue of whether people were married or divorced. The teachers on the weekends are lay people. The Anglicans adopted the method with the aim of changing nominal Christians into practising Christians. Those who belong to the "Cursillos" are involved in the follow-up biblical circles.

4. There was Liturgical Renewal and Diversity. Native rites and instruments were used. Spontaneity and participation were emphasised. There were more informal services, including "Youth Services"

For the poor communities
Radio programmes were developed and a simple and participative liturgy. Since all mission among the poor must have a social programme, social programmes were developed including kindergarten, day-care centres, mothers' clubs, and clubs for retired people, together with government social agencies or in partnership with World Vision.

Theology

To establish an evangelistic work in a nominal Christian country it is necessary, preliminarily, to recognise the nominal character of the country's Christianity, its syncretism and lack of commitment. One is not proselytising but carrying out evangelism, since people are being confronted for the first time in their lives with the Gospel. The situation is not substantially different from a non-Christian country.

Therefore, universalism and sacramentalism must be rejected as soteriological options. The Anglican mission in North East Brazil, since the beginning, took an evangelical option, trying to integrate both charismatic and non-charismatic evangelicals.

Challenged by the deteriorating social reality there came the awareness that mere First World evangelicalism was insufficient. It either had no social conscience or adopted a paternalistic approach to the poor. The impact of Liberation Theology with its many positive contributions could not be ignored. It helped people understand the social dimensions of the Gospel. But its liberal presuppositions were deeply rooted in the social gospel movement and it had no word of a deeper spiritual life. It only saw the Church as an avant-garde of the Kingdom, consisting of those who knew they were saved while others were saved but did not yet know it. This was not acceptable to evangelicals.

The main theological influence came to be the Holistic (Integral Mission) School, developed in the Continent by the Latin American Theological Fraternity in the last 20 years.

Obstacles

External
The Protestant Churches that were already established in the Region – almost all fundamentalist and legalistic – reacted against the presence of a more open Church. The Roman Catholic Church saw this openess and our liturgical emphasis as a menace, that could attract people who sympathized with the Gospel but, at the same time, had barriers against the narrow standards of traditional and pentecostal Protestantism.

Internal
Our distance and isolation in relation to the main concentration of Anglicans and the Church headquarters (4,000 km south), financial limitations and shortage of personnel have been obstacles which have exacted a heavy price.

But our major difficulty has been the antagonistic attitude against the evangelicals by part of the Church leadership. They feared the Northern part of the country becoming an evangelical "stronghold", a menace to the hegemony of the liberal-catholic tradition.

When Bishop Sherrill retired the Church Synod appointed a new Bishop from the South, giving a non-evangelical direction to the Dioceses. This has caused tense situations. The new candidates for Holy Orders have been ordered to stay apart from the evangelicals as a condition of their Ordination. No new project has been initiated in the last 5 years.

There is a hope that the Programme of the "Decade of Evangelism" will have a positive effect on the Church's attitude.

The Results

The evangelistic impulse of the initial project continues locally in the parishes whose ministers were trained in the old missionary spirit. After 15 years we have more than 2,000 Anglicans in North East Brazil; half of them are in Holy Trinity Parish. In Recife there is another parish and two missions (plus the Diocesan Office), one parish in Olinda city (also in Pernambuco State), one parish in Joao Pessoa (Paraiba State) and one parish and two missions in Salvador (Bahia State).

There is an Anglican "presence" in the region who have a positive image as viewed by society. Hundreds of people sympathize with our way and our message. They visit our churches and look for the opinions of our ministers.

From every main city in the Region come requests to start an Anglican mission. Unhappily it does not happen because of shortage of resources and lack of vision. We are convinced that all our effort has not been in vain.

Chapter Twelve

Chile: Evangelism in the 'Mink and Mercedes' Set

Alf Cooper

Introduction

Most missionary work in Chile has been done among the poor and the working class. Most of Chile's explosive Pentecostal church growth has taken place among these people. Pentecostal mission has been indigenous, self-propagating and by people without Bible college training. It involved much hard work in the early days of "sowing the seed" through persistent street preaching. For the Pentecostals, even church-going is an evangelistic activity. People march to church en masse, and stop to sing, preach, testify and pray for healings along the way. Worship is dynamic. This is not triumphalism, but simply triumph.

Earlier generations of Anglican missionaries also laboured in slums among the very poor. More recently however, the South American Missionary Society decided to try to reach into the more middle-class and prosperous areas. Today's evangelism is directed at the 'mink and mercedes' set. Hilary and I have been involved for four years in the plushest part of Santiago.

I never dreamt I would end up in a city. For me, mission had been a romantic idea of going to the poor and living in squalor among them, evangelizing and helping. But then God drew my attention to the wealthy professional areas where there are no churches.

The vision began in prayer and gradually emerged of churches which would grow continuously, through healthy growth principles inherent in their make-up, structures, programmes, lifestyle and national leadership.

Early attempts were not encouraging. The poor are so open to the love of Christ that preaching will get an immediate audience. In the middle-class context, preaching in public was a disaster. We began sketchboard evangelism, conducting questionnaires and opinion polls among affluent youth in shopping centres for the wealthy. Out of this came invitations into homes in high rise apartment blocks, which are otherwise virtually impossible to penetrate past the janitor. Eventually it was possible to aim to establish a house church on each floor of these apartment blocks.

A Church planted

After forming some house churches in this way, the Christians built a church building capable of holding 250 people. In a sense the building came before the people. The inside is light and attractive but very simple in contrast with the Roman Catholic churches. By now there are 380 new members, all of them new converts.

We have a church structured for mission rather than maintenance. One advantage in Chile is that since you start off with no church at all, you have to develop mission structures. Then growth results. Evangelism just happens continuously. After a church service, it spills over outside, in person to person conversation, barbecues and "food evangelism".

Among the congregation are neurologists, factory-owners, and bank managers. One is a multi-millionaire, who occasionally brings tithes, as he says "to put wheels on the gospel". The people are highly educated and very influential. Some have had previous careers in the upper ranks of drug dealing. Many come with all kinds of despair, emptiness and brokenness under the facade of their wealth. We spend a lot of time dealing with pastoral and spiritual problems and in the ministry of deliverance through prayer. We hold regular prayer clinics for prayer healing, e.g. for drug addicts. God has a wonderful healing love for even these people. When such people come to Christ, apart from the tremendous change in their own lives, there is a whole "golden seam of evangelism" behind them – i.e. their friends, acquaintances, business partners, etc. The most fruitful church growth comes by mining that seam behind each new convert.

We have used different methods. We have discarded evangelism that does not win people or add them to the Church. We have adopted the continuous, every member, sparkle and testimony dinner-party, answered prayer lifestyle evangelism that not only works but keeps on bringing people in all the year

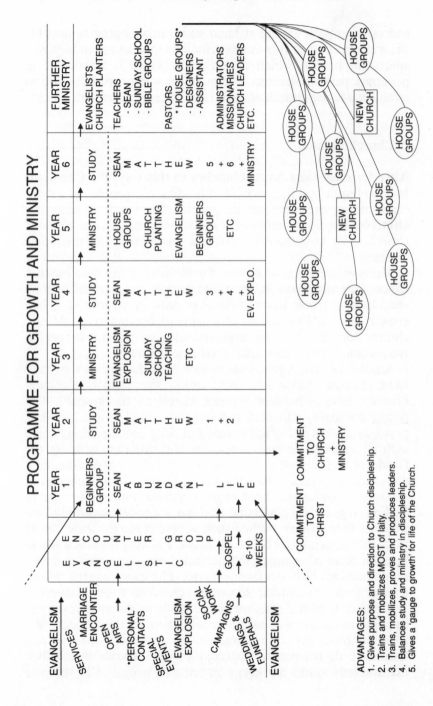

round, whether we are holding special evangelistic efforts or not. This evangelism only works when believers are excited about what is happening to them and in their church. That atmosphere happens when God is manifestly present in services, changed lives, big and small miracles. And the key to that is much prayer.

One method that really works is marriage encounter weekends. Sometimes as many as ten new Christian couples may arrive in church as a result on the following Sunday. But also all the normal range of church based activities – scouts, youth, and women's clubs have an evangelistic potential.

Discipleship

We place a high priority on initial discipleship. Initial discipling of a new believer shapes him or her for the rest of his or her life. A new believer wants to be taught how to live a real Christian life. The first year is the most important in the life of a new convert. We spend that year in basic Christian teaching and sorting out all kinds of personal and pastoral problems. In Beginners' Groups instruction is given on how to live, how to love their spouses, how to bring up their kids, how to avoid temptation at the office, and how to balance their monthly budgets. As they learn these, worship, fellowship and evangelism simply overflow.

Leadership Training

We bring the Bible college to the local church through Study by Extension for All Nations (SEAN) materials. For a period of six years with new converts, we follow a pattern of alternating a year of study (through SEAN), with a year of practical ministry, e.g. Sunday School teaching, Evangelism Explosion, leading house groups and planting churches. Such a programme gives purpose and direction to church discipleship; trains and mobilizes most of the laity; proves and produces leaders; gives balanced study and ministry in discipleship and gives a guage for growth for the life of the church.

Even if the programme never quite works out as neatly as it is intended to, we still see every year a new batch of students and workers in training move along the assembly line. Once out the other side they are regarded as responsible workers within the Church, leading house-groups and other ministries in the Church.

Leadership Growth

We have to produce future leaders from scratch so we have had to find ways of training them without Bible Colleges. We find that the school of the local congregation goes a long way to teach them most of the useful things they need to know in order to be effective in ministry. Learning on the job, beside the pastor, or sent out on special pastoring or church-planting errands, they pick up the essentials of ministry. How vital to see, experience and do healing, prayer counselling, demonic deliverance, planning a service, preparing a church retreat, helping to plan next year's programme or a day of fasting and prayer. They seem to absorb more than just the facts, but also the authority and spiritual power to get the job done. Supplementing this kind of learning with the more formal (recently developed) central diploma courses where they can discuss good teaching in a context wider than their local church, greatly enriches them if they are already involved in ministry. From the start we tell them they will be the future pastors, evangelistis, church-planters, and teachers in the Church. They seem to grow into their calling.

Social involvement

We aim to break down barriers in society. Within the Church, Christ is bridging the social divisions in Chile. He also heals the divisions between the extremists on the left and right wings among Christians. The only way we could begin was in one sense by favouring the rich, which sounds contrary to what is supposed to happen. But, methodologically, it was necessary for us to start by having meetings which culturally and socially would make it comfortable for them to hear and receive the Gospel.

I preach to my congregation that from them will come the social reformers of Chile. They need to get involved with the needs, problems and injustices of society. I do not give them a pre-packaged idea of how they must do it. But I leave them in no doubt that they have the responsibility for social justice in the country today.

Exposure to the problems is part of this. For example, we encourage wealthy women in the Church to go to the soup kitchens in the slums with food and fuel. They have to step out of their rich ghetto and actually go and get involved with the poor. So they go and see. This is not to preach a pre-packaged liberation theology. I say to them: "Go with Jesus in your heart and see what Christ says to you there."

We have not taken a high level political stand in Chile, but rather seek to help practically where we can. Our main role is to preach reconciliation rather than confrontation. If we actively got involved in politics to the extent of advocating violent revolution, we would probably be thrown out. Chile is hungrier for Christ than for upheaval in politics. I can understand the pressures, the suffering and the frustration that cause some Christian groups to opt for violent struggle. But I cannot see Jesus leading people into violence.

Growth

As a church begins to reach a fair stage of numerical growth, and a certain maturity (a hundred or so members after four or five years), we consider budding off a new church, moving some of the leaders with part of the congregation to the new area (geographical factors help decide who moves) to start the new church. This worked successfully in the case of the Providencia church which after six years helped start the Las Condes church. Las Condes, in turn, is now looking to plant a new church over the next few years in a nearby section of the Barrio Alto called La Reina. Each new church adopts the same growth principles they are used to in their previous church and thereby healthy growing churches are multiplied.[1]

Footnotes

1. This case study was presented at the conference *in absentia* through video presentations of a lecture at All Nations Christian College, and a BBC interview for a documentary on "Missionaries". These have been transcribed and edited together with an article first published in the EFAC Bulletin in Pentecost 1988.

Chapter Thirteen

England: Evangelism on a New Housing Estate

Andrew Knowles

What?

St Andrew's Church Goldsworth Park is a congregation of about 170 committed adults based in a new church at the centre of a housing estate. It is an area where cost of housing and commuting time to London finds a balance, with the result that many people, both men and women, are away from their homes and the estate during the day. An evening meal and a couple of hours watching television all too easily account for any free time.

Where?

Goldsworth Park in Surrey, England, is a large housing development. In 1960 the area (about one square mile) was nursery land. In the ensuing years it has become 'home' for 12,500 people. It has been described as the largest development of its kind in Western Europe – its kind being a single development which mixes both private and local authority ('council') homes in a ratio of 4:1.

Who?

The residents of Goldsworth Park are a mixture of the newly-married, the newly-born, and the newly-retired. Most are white middle-class, living in pairs or small family units. In one district there is a significant Moslem minority group – and the school in that area has between 12 and 17 different nationalities represented among the children.

The range of accommodation, from blocks of flats to terraced houses, and from two-bedroomed bungalows to four-bedroomed homes, encourages a community of young families and 'young' retired folk. There are very few teenagers, and only a temporary cabin for youth activities. Many people have moved house but stayed in the area. Turnover was about 26% per annum until the current situation of high interest rates and falling house prices brought removals to a standstill.

The development has been built up through dozens of 'phases' – a 'phase' being anything from a pocket of eight retirement bungalows to a group of roads with hundreds of homes. The fact that many people live in a close or cul-de-sac enables young mothers particularly to meet each other, but can pitch the elderly into almost intolerable loneliness. Because of the rising cost of living, many mothers seek employment – leaving their children with child-minders during the day. There is a dearth of people with time, energy and inclination to care for the elderly.

Most people are affluent by world standards, but feel short of money. Rising mortgage rates have caused considerable stress, and many people have some kind of credit card debt or hire purchase commitment. Many homes have more than one television, a video recorder, a micro-wave oven, a dish-washer, a washing machine, and a second car. Even the poorest homes have a television, and probably a video.

People are fashionably dressed and able to afford convenience foods. Buying clothes, eating out, or ordering a 'take-away' meal, are popular forms of relaxation. The most likely economy is to stay at home rather than go away for a holiday, or take a series of shorter 'week-end' breaks during the year.

Not everyone is affluent. The elderly, many of them living in 'sheltered', warden-supervised accommodation, are not well off; and some 'council' areas of the estate are clearly socially and materially deprived. At one time an area of 600 homes, known as 'Lakeview', accounted for 12% of the social services' resources for the whole of Woking (pop 87,600).

The Church reflects the age-structure of the estate population, with a predominance of young parents and young children. The 'missing' segments are people in their 50s – and teenagers.

A sample of 98 households within the congregation shows:

Under 5	5–12	13–18	18–30	30–40	40–50	50–60	60–70	Over 70
35	50	12	41	43	30	7	22	15

How?

Sharing the Life.
Andrew and Diane Knowles moved to Goldsworth Park estate with their 18-month-old daughter Hannah, in November 1977. Andrew was curate of the 'parent' church of St John's Woking, under the leadership of the Vicar, the Rev Jimmie Song. Jimmie's vision was that the curate and his family should live on the new development and share its life, while retaining a life-line in the less exposed and more familiar responsibilities of the parish church. An estate house was purchased, with a garage converted to make a study/meeting room. First contact with fellow residents was through helping each other move in, and through the Residents' Association.

A small housegroup was formed fairly quickly, meeting weekly and occasionally sharing an informal communion service on a Sunday. It proved very difficult to 'split' the group when it grew to 8 or 10 members, and there was little shared vision of being engaged in 'church planting'. Even when the 'Goldsworth' group grew to some 25 families, it seemed a daunting (and unnecessary) task to establish a new parish with its own Church Centre.

Diane Knowles started a 'Mums & Toddlers' group, which was exclusively for the residents of the new estate, but met in the hall of the parish church. The Toddler Group began to mark Christmas and Easter with short 'events'. An older man, Ken Gough, formed the 'Goldsworth Afternoon Club' for retired folk. It met on the premises of the parish church, but moved out when 'Bingo' was forbidden.

The formation of Toddler Groups and a Retired Folk's Club was an early expression of community involvement. Indeed, it was found that there could be no communication until there was community. It was noticeable that people were unsettled, having moved away from family and friends and finding themselves in an environment without shops, buses, telephones, footpaths, or established gardens. One odd statistic was that, of the babies born in 1979, 14 out of 16 were boys – almost as though the community was subconsciously recovering from a war.

The Residents' Association
A glimmer of light shone from the Residents' Association, which

established itself through 'phase reps', to fight the battles for street lights and good drainage. Social events were few and poorly attended, and to this day the residents of Goldsworth Park have declined to be very sociable. The Residents' (now 'Community') Association still struggles with lack of support, and its future looks bleak.

The Bishop of Stepney, the Rt Rev Jim Thompson, has observed that the building of houses without community facilities is a blasphemy – a denial of the way God intended us to live. Goldsworth Park was an 'instant town', but without shops, pubs, churches, chapels or meeting halls: a non-community of boxed nuclear families, removed from familiar relationships, preoccupied with possessions, and short of space and money.

In 1979 Andrew Knowles became editor of the Residents' Newsletter, and other Christians served as committee members and 'phase reps'. However, it was clear that the existing members of the committee felt in danger of being taken over by the Church, and there was a pulling-back on both sides. When it came to planning accommodation for Church and Community, it was felt that 'good fences make good neighbours' and that we should build separately. Meanwhile, members of the embrionic church were influential in the formation of a 'Goldsworth Action Group' which challenged the commercial interests of the Woking Chamber of Commerce, raised a petition for a supermarket on the new estate, and took the whole issue to Public Enquiry – with success.

The Formation of a Parish
In due course two schools were built on the estate, and it proved possible to hold occasional services – Harvest, Christmas, Easter and Mothering Sunday. These were well-attended by the Mums & Toddlers, and the 'Afternoon Club'. From Whit Sunday 25th May 1980 services were held every Sunday. A year later, on April 1st 1981, Goldsworth Park became an independent parish, and on 23rd May Andrew Knowles was instituted as Vicar.

All this took some time, as the two 'parent' parishes (St Mary the Virgin Horsell and St John's Woking) were both eager for the patronage, as was the Bishop of Guildford, the Rt Rev David Brown. In the end Bishop David secured the patronage, and offered Andrew the incumbency, providing he wore a stole (to represent 'middle ground'), used 'Hymns Ancient & Modern

Revised', and didn't swamp the bookstall with evangelical literature! Of these requirements, the first was acceptable (the stole as a symbol of the yoke of the Gospel), the second impossible (the first set of hymn books, 'Christian Praise', were retrieved from the dustbin of a neighbouring church), and the third irrelevant (most of the congregation were not in the habit of buying or reading books – and Andrew kept his behind a curtain to keep the atmosphere of his study less threatening).

Appropriate Worship
From the beginning, the ethos of the services was friendly and informal. Some of the informality quickly gave way to a clearer 'Anglican' style – as though the unfamiliar surroundings of a school needed balancing by familiar robes and liturgy. But the services were called 'Something for Everyone', and there was a variety of content, style, and contributors.

There was a tension between the 'traditional' Anglicans who expected to perpetuate their churchmanship, and the effervescent 'charismatics' who shared camps and conferences with the 'house church' movement, and wanted 'all things new'. An early sermon series covered the Gospel of Mark. 'Christian Praise' was replaced by a home-made service book, which incorporated the Alternative Service Book liturgy with familiar hymns, new songs, and favourite prayers.

To seek to reach the socially-deprived area of 'Lakeview', we worked to publicise a 'Carol Sing-in' one Christmas. Of the 600 homes leafleted, only one family came. Another attempt to serve this area took the form of establishing an evening service at the local 'Sythwood' school, and conducting 'hymns and prayers' for the elderly in their 'sheltered' accommodation. The evening service never drew a congregation of any size, and became a 'second' Sunday service for keen Christians – and a training ground for Ordinands.

To counter the tendency to become a 'ghetto' Anglican congregation, a third service was started in October 1982: the 'Sunday Special'. This was for families with young children, lasted half an hour, and incorporated songs, stories, dressing-up, and quizzes. A 'treasure box' containing a surprise object was a popular feature in the early days. The service had an added advantage of giving opportunity for more people to lead and speak, and some future Readers and Ordinands emerged at this time.

The 'Sunday Special' was held in the Beaufort Middle School at 9.30 am and sometimes included a church parade or baptism. On such occasions attendance could rise to over 100, but plummet to 12 the following week. Not many of the established church members were in sympathy with the new service, and tended to leave Andrew to get on with it. Even after 18 months, in March 1984, there was a 'Sunday Special' with only 12 adults and 9 children present.

A turning-point seemed to come with the advent of a new Reader, Chris Holloway, and an Ordinand, Bruce Nicole. They formed a housegroup for adult teaching during the week and, with their wives, created a children's 'story time' on Sunday mornings.

By April 1988, the attendance at the two morning services at Beaufort Middle School ('Sunday Special' at 9.30 and Family Communion at 10.45) was about equal, with some 80 adults and 30 children at each. After that the attendance equation seemed to be governed by the 'goldfish bowl' principle (the amount of space available) and the staff ratio (Andrew Knowles was the sole full-time minister). 'Church Growth' theory favours 10% of the seats to be empty if newcomers are to feel there's a place for them. At the same time statistics show that a single church leader can only relate meaningfully to about 120 adults. These observations were borne out in Goldsworth Park.

Occasions the Community Comes to the Church

Baptisms
One of the main ways in which the community looks to the Church is for baptism, especially of children. The church on Goldsworth Park has always had a fairly open baptism policy, preferring to put energy into saying 'Yes' to enquirers and preparing them positively, rather than plunging into lengthy, irritable, and sometimes incomprehensible discussion by saying 'No'.

An enquiry about baptism or christening of a child will often come by telephone. This is met with an invitation to come to 'Sunday Special' one morning, where they will be introduced to members of the baptism team and invited to an evening of preparation. Preparation evenings are held every month, and include a slide presentation and discussion in pairs and small groups. Members of the baptism team handle the hospitality and contribute to the discussion. The Gospel is helpfully introduced through the 'Bridge'. This evening is followed with a home visit from one of the Team, accompanied by a Christian neighbour who is encouraged to keep in touch.

This basic approach has been played with many variations (involvement of house groups in the hospitality, enlistment of prayer partners for each family) and occasional collapse. In practice the team members, with young families of their own, have found the work arduous, especially with the pressure of people simply 'wanting the baby done'. Even the staunchest team members need to be relieved of the responsibility after about two years.

The following table shows the number of adults and children baptized each year since 1980, together with an indication of their subsequent commitment.

	ADULTS						CHILDREN					
YEAR	TOTAL	C	N	CE	MA	NFC	TOTAL	C	N	CE	MA	NFC
1980	–	–	–	–	–	–	31	1	12	2	8	8
1981	1	1	–	–	–	–	44	7	9	3	27	–
1982	–	–	–	–	–	–	53	9	11	2	29	2
1983	–	–	–	–	–	–	44	3	21	6	12	2
1984	6	4	2	2	–	–	61	6	10	2	2	41
1985	10	2	5	3	–	–	44	9	10	1	3	21
1986	–	–	–	–	–	–	47	7	9	2	–	29
1987	4	1	1	1	(Died)	–	40	8	13	1	2	16
1988	2	2	–	–	–	–	45	11	15	–	3	16
1989	3	2	1				94	23	21	3	4	7

C   = Congregation
N   = No Contact
CE = Nominal Members
MA = Moved Away
NFC = No Further contact

Weddings
The desire for a 'traditional' wedding means that many couples look for an old (and photogenic) church setting for their marriage service. Before Goldsworth Park had its own church building, weddings were conducted in one of the neighbouring churches, at the rate of about 18 each year. With the provision of a modern

building, the requests for weddings have dropped dramatically – to about 5 a year.

Preparation of couples takes place through three weekly meetings: one to discuss practical arrangements, another to outline the nature of Christian marriage and introduce the service, and a third to explore 'Hidden Baggage' (the experiences, hopes and fears we smuggle into our relationship). These evenings are run by a small team and are felt to be an excellent approach – but without discernable fruit spiritually.

Funerals

On a young estate there are relatively few funerals – between 12 and 20 each year. There have been a number of 'cot deaths', and in one year as many as half the funerals were for babies. Again, these are seen as opportunities for loving Christian care rather than overt evangelism. Some bereaved parents have responded to God in their need, while others have firmly shut him out. One joy is that, as and when they have another child, there is further opportunity to build the relationship.

Funerals for adults are generally well-appreciated by the family, who are grateful for an understanding and personal approach. A relative, especially the bereaved partner, will sometimes attend church for a Sunday or two after the service. Sometimes friends and neighbours have become aware of the church for the first time and subsequently become committed members. It is generally considered that Andrew Knowles, as the clergyman called to help, makes good initial contact ('Andy, you're the master of the 20-minute friendship'), but the on-going support has been patchy and ineffective.

Ways the Church serves the Community

Helping Community 'happen'

A new estate is manifestly a non-community, without history, accepted values, mutual knowledge, or clear identity. The Church in such a situation has a strong identity and can serve as an active agent in helping the community form. On a broad front, St Andrew's has helped a lot of things 'happen' and, under God, made Goldsworth Park a better place to live.

Schools
There are three schools on the estate: Beaufort County First School, Beaufort County Middle School (next door to each other), and a combined Sythwood First & Middle School. Although none of them are 'church' schools, Andrew Knowles has been welcome to conduct assemblies on a weekly basis, and there have been one or two successful holiday clubs for the children. Involvement with the schools has developed to the extent that church members are now extensively involved in teaching, helping in classes, supporting the parent-teachers' association, and serving as school governors. Here is an open door for further contact with children and parents who were first known to the Church through baptism. Recently a group met to pray for the schools, with an exhilarating sense of the Lord's presence and purpose.

The Elderly
With the provision of a Church Centre we have a place where the elderly can come and meet friends, as well as have coffee or lunch. There is also a 'Drop-in' Centre adjacent to our building, known as 'Strollers', which is permanently available to the elderly and disabled. We have recently acquired a minibus, the 'Flying Dolphin', to act as a mini social centre for the elderly and disabled around the estate, and to assist in transporting them.

Strategic Service
A few of our church members are strategically active in the community. One is a County Councillor and another a Borough Councillor. One of our Churchwardens, Mrs Pat Stubbs, is a very effective Community Social Worker for 'Lakeview'.

'Christian Listeners'
In recent months we have established a group of trained counsellors, called 'Christian Listeners'. Our hope is that they will interface with the local Health Centre and Community Services to provide caring and helpful support for people who need someone to talk to.

Aspects of Evangelism
Accessible Worship
Although the teaching at St Andrew's is that 'worship' is the

offering of the whole of our lives, everywhere and all the time, a major aspect of evangelism has been to establish 'user-friendly' worship occasions. A very considerable part of the growth of the church has been through the provision of services that families with young children can attend, and in which all ages can participate.

A Church Centre

Similarly, the building of a Church Centre, opened in September 1988, has provided a place for teaching and fellowship, and a base for mission. The main worship area is upstairs and seats 240. Downstairs is a lounge which serves as a coffee shop and restaurant ('Open House') several days per week, but easily converts to accommodate four Toddler Groups, an afternoon club for the elderly (the '0−6−0' Club) and an assortment of other activities. There is a small Chapel for daily prayer and small services.

Door-to-door Visitation

In 1977−8 each home on the estate was visited with the help of small teams from neighbouring churches. The idea was to welcome people to the area 'in the name of Christ'. It was felt that this was a useful exercise in terms of discovering who had moved into the area and whether they had any 'church' background. We weren't geared-up to meet the needs and requests we met − for the formation of uniformed organisations, support for the housebound, and so on.

As time has gone by, many structures and organisations have been established from the point of view of community service. Door-to-door visitation for faith-sharing has proved useful for identifying fellow-Christians, but unwelcome to many homes. The local experience of door-step callers is that, if they are not Jehovah's Witnesses, they are conducting surveys or trying to sell something. Such callers are felt to be intrusive.

Publicity

Our first attempts at publicity were very 'home-made', but effective all the same. A photocopier proved to be a one of the most important investments we made. Reproducing short letters in Andrew's own handwriting helped keep communication personal and informal in a setting which was strange and impersonal for many. We also used children's drawings for our artwork, which worked well on a young estate.

Twelve years on, we have launched a community paper, called 'Centrepiece', which we deliver to every home. The approach and impression is more professional and sophisticated, in keeping with the present mood of the estate. Delivery is approached by areas – each with an area manager and team. This has potential for increasing our regular contact with our neighbours, as well as giving a means of interpreting the estate to itself and sharing the Good News in a variety of ways through addressing particular issues.

'Evangelism Explosion'

We ran a course of 'Evangelism Explosion' in 1979-80, with two trainers and two teams. There is a high time commitment (17 weeks) on these courses, which proved too much for the young couples taking part. Nevertheless, we saw a couple converted through this programme who, although they have moved away from the area, have proved committed and useful Christians.

Billy Graham '89

Although we were very much on the fringe of the Billy Graham Mission of 1986 (attending 'Live-link' in a desultory way), we were better set up to participate in 1989. Attendance at 'Live-link' meetings, together with coaches to meetings at Crystal Palace and Wembley, had a marked impact at the time. We had 50 commitments or enquirers (twice the average for other local churches), including some recommitments from within our congregation and commitments by our children.

Student Mission

We were visited by a team of a dozen students from Ridley Hall Cambridge, in September 1989. In the course of a week they serviced 'business breakfasts', school assemblies, an 'after-school club', some door-to-door visits and evangelistic supper parties. They also performed street theatre in the shopping precinct on the Saturday afternoon and contributed fully to Sunday services. In retrospect this mission provided a welcome 'freshen-up' for our congregation, together with a very significant impact on the schools. Goldsworth homes proved too small for the kind of supper parties envisaged, and the team members probably didn't have the skills or experience to handle such occasions. The opportunities in the schools are such that they could absorb such a team permanently.

Chapter Fourteen

Canada: Evangelism in an affluent secular city

St. John's Church (Shaughnessy), Vancouver, Canada: 1979 to 1990

Harry Robinson and Ruth Matheson

Vancouver

Vancouver is a city surrounded by great natural beauty – mountains on the north, ocean in the midst and to the west, and a large river to the south. In the winter, there is very little snow at sea level and the temperature is relatively mild (seldom below 0°C) so that you could spend the morning on the mountains skiing and the afternoon on the Inlet sailing. People are very serious about their leisure time activities (there is even night skiing so that people can go after work).

Canadians are rather diffident people, conservative and polite. They live in the shadow of the United States. When North Americans come to live in Canada, they are rather perplexed by the way we do things. They seem to live with even more hype than do Canadians who have enough as it is (they wear a mask of efficiency, want things to be done yesterday, complain about trifles, etc.). There is an undercurrent of anger in the country. We are involved in debates at the national level about abortion, about our deficit, and about the very integrity and unity of the country itself.

Vancouver seems to be on the outer edge of the world, quite out of the main-stream of the world's commerce. Geographically it is isolated from the rest of the country. It lies on the San Andreas Fault and a very major earthquake (measuring 9 or more on the Richter Scale) is predicted to occur within the next 250 years. When a major earthquake happens somewhere else in the world, the residents are somewhat anxious about Vancouver's situation but then carry on in their hedonistic lifestyle. Contradictions abound. It is a nuclear free city (and nuclear powered ships are excluded from the harbour) on the one hand, but on the other pollution is increasing as the number of cars on the road rises.

It is a city in transition from medium size to large. It is on the Pacific Rim and is thus attractive to Chinese immigrants from Hong Kong. The climate is the most temperate in all of Canada and so middle aged, wealthy Eastern Canadians, tired of hard, cold winters are attracted to this part of the country. In the past few years, the significant influx of these two wealthy groups of people has pushed house prices up and made rental accommodation very hard to come by and quite expensive for those on low and fixed incomes.

Many residents of Vancouver have a cottage out of town to which they go on weekends and for the summer – either in the mountains or on the Gulf Islands. Even people considered lower middle class have been able to afford such holiday accommodation.

The City and the Word of God

The city of Vancouver has many tall buildings in the down-town area. And our congregation operates from a small church that is dwarfed by them. So when I talk of evangelism, there is a certain importance to the relationship between the size of me and the size of them. But I am greatly encouraged by Jacques Ellul who says that the city is the counter creation. God has created a world for us to live in. But because we are dissatisfied with the world that was given to us we created our own counter creation, our own world.

In the world God is God and in our world man is God. Man can be anonymous, lustful, dishonest and greedy. He can be anything he likes because he makes the rules. So Jacques Ellul says that the city is the place where man is God. He likes to have a few temples, shrines and a few historical places. But these are mostly empty and ineffective in really affecting the whole life of the city.

Vancouver is considered by most Vancouver people as the loveliest place on earth. So when we first went to Vancouver , the first question we were asked was whether we liked Vancouver. I said "Do you think Jonah liked Nineveh?". Less than 5% of people have any church connection at all. A missionary came to raise funds in Vancouver for his work in the Solomon Islands. When he was asked how many people in Solomon Islands go to church he said 95%. So it was nice that we were able to take an offering for his mission in the Solomon Islands. That is partly because that means we do not have to take seriously the mission we have to Vancouver.

The city is a declaration of humanity's independence of God. It is there and it is hard and it is real and it is very attractive. It confers on people status, rewards, and wealth; it provides art, sophistication, social belonging and all those things. It meets so many of people's needs. But the question is whether the Christians in the city are like the person in the Volkswagen driving up to the person in the Solid Gold Cadillac saying "I have got something that you haven't got." What that something is is not immediately obvious.

In the city what comes through people like us, the Church, is the word of God and the word of God is completely confounding to the city. They simply don't know what to do with it. What they try to do with it is to get historians, sociologists, and psychologists and try to reduce the word *of* God to a word *from a* god along with all sorts of other words and all sorts of other gods and so they can dismiss it. They find *the* word from the *living* God very hard to read, difficult to comprehend and too complicated. Many of them have a familiarity with it which breeds contempt.

So the word of God coming up against the city is the essential ingredient of what has to happen. You really have nothing else to bring up against the city. The fact is that the word of God opens our heart to the awareness that God knows who we are. The Word of God can reveal to the city what it is. The Word of God is absolutely essential to the city because it is only way the city can come to identity itself. The preaching and teaching of Word of God is very important to the city. The ministry of the sacraments can only come after that has been effectively done.

The Word of God does what the city constitutionally denies. It says that there is another reality. The city understands itself to be only reality. These clean streets, these tall buildings, this commerce, this banking, this law, and this industry and what it has achieved is what life is all about. Finding some meaning and purpose for life within the process is what life is all about. We have in our congregation a man who has been a captain of industry and been extremely successful. He has an accounting firm, retained only for the purpose of maximising how much the company can give him and how much he can take home without being taxed beyond endurance. His whole life is based on his place in the city. His company has said you are through on June 1st. He is 65 years old and he has been told it is all over. He has derived the meaning of his life from the city. The only meaning he has is in his relationship to the city.

The irresistable force meets the immovable object when the Word of God comes up against the city. The great drama of history is that this happens. A good illustration of it is in a book from a foremost Canadian writer. He describes the Jews' inability to build. He said they couldn't build a city. Even when they did try and build a temple they had to import the workers to come from another place to do it because they could not do it. Jonah went to Nineveh, a great city, which took three days to walk across. Those people had produced this tremendous city. For almost twenty centuries nobody has even known where that city was. All that Jews produced was a book. It is a wonderful contrast when you see what the situation is between the city and the book which is the Word of God.

Inevitably in the end the book is going to be there as a witness to the city which will fail. In a city like Vancouver with our cultural pluralism, and our multi-cultural mosaic when everything is true, all religions are acceptable. All religion is equally true and all religion is equally false. So everything is dismissed. The only truth is that there is no truth. The ultimate idea is no idea. That kind of basic contradiction forces you to recognise that this city is only a very temporary phenomenon. It is not an enduring city. It is going to pass and be forgotten like the rest. That is the nature of the city.

Into that city comes an eternal word, which must ultimately transcend the city. Lesslie Newbigin says that what is required is a paradigm shift: it is not possible to get from Newtonian physics to Einstein's physics by developing Newtonian physics. You have to start from somewhere else altogether. The city of man can never become the eternal city. Something else has to happen, no matter how hard we work at developing the life of the city creating the perfect environment for humanity to live in. No matter how great our goals, how great our architects, our sociologists, social workers and all the rest, no matter what our law courts can do, what our commerce can do, what our industry can do, you cannot get there from here. The ultimate reality for man is not going to be the product of the city.

The city is here and now. In the city you are inevitably dead before you die. Because the city cannot do that much for you. The city cannot help you. So into the city comes the paradigm shift. All that the city can do with Jesus Christ is to crucify him. There is nothing else it can do with him. For any city the inescapable logic is that it is good that this man should die for the city. Jesus represents a possibility that we cannot incorporate into the city. He is intolerable to us. The city says that and acts that out in a million of ways.

In this situation, we begin our evangelism not with the necessity of the crucifixion of Jesus Christ, but with his resurrection: that something has happened and because it has happened then this all ultimately must derive its meaning from the fact that Jesus Christ has risen from dead. There is a totally new creation, a new reality. There is a Gospel that reaches to every person and every place and every corner of the globe. Just as one comes to Africa and sees how Christian Faith has been wonderfully refined and focused by its encounter with Islam so there is a wonderful way in which the Christian Gospel is refined and focused as it comes up against militant secularism. It requires that we do not carry any baggage. That is all stripped away in the encounter with militant secularism. If you have got a gospel you must be very sure of it and clear about it.

Vinay Samuel's paper in this volume tells a most moving story of the mass migration of people who were suffering all sorts of deprivation and poverty; how the Christians were able to move in there and negotiate with the municipal authority, and get water supplies and all they help they needed. But in a city like Vancouver we cannot do that. The Christian community is the offscouring; we cannot help anybody. People do not need housing. Basically that is not the way the Gospel takes a foothold in Vancouver. The Gospel can only take a foothold in Vancouver by saying there is a hope in a city that has lost hope; there is purpose in a city that has abandoned meaning; and there is life in a city that is committed to death.

I had fifteen years in a slum parish in Toronto which was called the poor man's church. Then I came out and had almost twelve years in what has been called the rich man's church. And as far as I am concerned the poor man is much wealthier than the rich man because wealth is very demanding and extremely deceiving. I have a great deal of sympathy for the wealthy because they are so deceived by the City and all that it affords and all that wealth can give. In preaching the Gospel in the City you are undermining the whole basis of a person's prestige, standing and social place by saying that this wealth does not ultimately count for anything. You are setting up a terrible contradiction in a person's life. Mink and Mercedes do not go that far. They do not answer that many questions.

The Church

There are two universities and two theological colleges in Vancouver. The largest university (the University of British Columbia) and the two theological colleges which are on the UBC campus are only 7 miles away from St. John's Church. The Vancouver School of Theology is the theological college officially recognized by the Diocese of New Westminster. It is an amalgamation of three denominations – the United Church of Canada, the Anglican Church of Canada and the Presbyterian Church of Canada. It is liberal in its theology. The other theological college is Regent College which is evangelical in theology. It actually has more Anglican students in attendance than does Vancouver School of Theology, but is not recognized by the Diocese.

Vancouver was a predominantly Anglo-Saxon city and the Anglican Church brought to the West Coast the liturgical order, the Church history, English loyalty and Anglican folk religion.[1] The clergy of the Diocese have been, and still are, predominantly English and Irish and there is a colonial loyalty to Anglicanism which would probably not even be understood in England.

St John's

The Parish of St. John's is in Shaughnessy Heights, named after a director of the Canadian Pacific Railway (CPR). The actual land in the community was once owned by the CPR to house their executives and families in Vancouver which was the Western Terminal of the trans-continental railway.

The Diocese is called New Westminster. The first cathedral was in that city, just east of Vancouver. In 1924 Bishop de Pencier, recognized that the importance of New Westminster was fading and that Vancouver owned the future. So he bought property for the See House in Shaughnessy, considering it to be central to the growing City of Vancouver. In the basement of the See House a chapel was built and a Sunday School begun in 1925. Subsequently, a frame church and hall were built. Then in the early 1950's an imposing all cement Scandanavian style church and a huge hall were built when Church life was booming and Sunday Schools were very active.

I came to Vancouver from 15 years in a militantly low-church, protestant, evangelical parish in Toronto which is 3,000 miles to the east. I am a life-long Anglican, married to a life-long Anglican. I had served in 5 Anglican parishes since my ordination prior to coming to Vancouver.

The attendance at St. John's had fallen off very badly. A great many of the affluent and influential people on the parish list were more like patrons than parishioners. The high points in the parish's year were the Easter and Christmas music. Because of falling income and a large plant to maintain, Wednesday night Bingo, a Saturday Night dance, a rummage sale and a Christmas bazaar were important sources of income.

St. John's Church was a beautiful church and a lovely property in a prestigious neighbourhood with a beautiful boys' choir and a very costly organ and all the outward signs of Anglicanism – cross, candles, vested choir, crucifer, servers, wardens' wands, and a tabernacle for the reserved sacrament. My commitment was to maintain Prayer Book worship and doctrine and Biblical and evangelistic preaching, not to change the outward signs of Anglican cult.

I had been converted in a parish church Bible class in a church where I had been baptized, confirmed and made a deacon, where my grandparents had belonged and were buried in the graveyard. My conversion brought me into contact with the Inter-School Christian Fellowship at High School, the Inter-Varsity Christian Fellowship at University and the Inter-Varsity summer camps. So I encountered and was very much influenced by evangelical-ism in the Anglican Church. I subsequently spent one seminary year at Oak Hill College in London, England and two years at Wycliffe College in Toronto, Canada.

So, when I came to St. John's I had been very influenced by evangelicalism and was deeply committed to Anglicanism historically, emotionally, and theologically. I had, and still have, a perhaps irrational, but deeply rooted loyalty to Anglicanism.[2]

It was very tramautic to arrive in this parish where word got ahead that I was an evangelical and people in parish had never heard of an evangelical. The President of the Sanctuary Guild took a dictionary to the next meeting of the Sanctuary Guild to try and explain it was not contagious, whatever it was. At an early vestry meeting one man got up in a fury and said to me "You are nothing but an evangelical." His understanding was that this was some form of prostitution of the Christian Faith.

My chief conviction was that Prayer Book worship and Biblical teaching and preaching would be central to my ministry. I bought St. Matthew's Gospel in the Good News Version for the congregation to use and began to preach my way through from cover to cover. Baptisms, funerals, weddings and home visiting gave me vital points of contact with the community.

In the first years of my ministry, there was a Monday Church Club rather than a Sunday School because so many families were out of town on weekends. The present situation is different.

The youth work needed to be established and built up from the foundations. A young woman with the gifts for doing that came to work with the teenagers – getting them into Bible studies, taking them on summer work trips and adventures and getting them all together once a week on a Friday night. She found a good group of leaders to work with the kids. Unlike some other denominations, we didn't go for numbers; we wanted to make disciples, to establish young people in the Faith. Our present youth worker was one of the teenagers in that original youth group work.

Confirmation preparation for both youth and adults has been an important place for people to become Christians over the years. Year by year, we have had a small but significant number of students from Regent College as active members of St. John's helping with the youth work or the Bible study groups or working here as interns.

Bible Study groups were virtually unheard of in St. John's before I came. I started off with a mid week Bible Study to which

12 or 15 came. Then during Lent, home groups were started and over the years more and more people have joined a home group, although we are a long way from even half of the parish membership being involved in a Bible study prayer group.

"A Week In The Life Of The Parish" was a programme that ran during the first six years that I was in the parish. It was helpful to those who participated and helped to get them more involved in the life of the parish and to have a broader understanding of the parish work.

Some women in the parish had become Christians through the Bible Study Fellowship before I came to the Parish. They wanted some of their friends to participate in Bible study, but in a more informal and less structured way than that offered by the Bible Study Fellowship. So, a women's Bible study was begun in one of the lovely homes in the neighbourhood. Through that study more women came to Faith. Some of their husbands became Christians after them so we started a Men's Bible study group, initially known as the Candadian Underwriters Association which meets down town in a hotel. Now 20 to 30 men meet weekly in the Church hall for breakfast and study. This has been an essential part of their growth in the Christian Faith, and in fellowship with other Christians.

A parish mission has taken place about every two or three years with a special speaker. Sometimes the mission has been for children, sometimes for adults and has been held over a weekend or over the course of a full week. Our purpose is that people will come to know Jesus Christ, not that they will participate in a great spectacle. So people have become Christians by ones, twos and threes and many when given opportunities during the missions or in epilogue services after a Sunday service.

The first annual parish weekend took place in 1979 in a hotel so that people who would be uncomfortable without the usual amenities could come and hear and meet Christians and bring their non-Christian spouses or friends. Only in the past 4 years have we been able to run family camps. We tried to run them earlier but there was no interest.

I started an evening service in January 1979 and there were about half a dozen of us in the congregation. The service was simple, the Scriptures were preached, there was informal music and an informal coffee hour afterwards. It was a training ground in the early years for lay assistants who have since gone on to be ordained Anglican clergy, both men and women. Our curate has taken responsibility for the service. 200 to 250 attend (the numbers fluctuate according to the university term).

Bible studies were not cancelled if there was just a handful of people in attendance. The message that came across was, "Bible study is important. You are important. If you want to come, there will be a Bible study." This is at variance with the attitude sometimes encountered that if there are only a handful of people, it's not worth running the programme. Numbers matter more than persons in some evangelical circles.

Quite a strong contingent of Inter-Varsity Christian Fellowship staff members belong to the congregation. We have sent many children and teenagers to Pioneer Camps run by Inter-Varsity.

Evangelism: Sowing the Seed in Burnt Over Territory

St. John's seems to have become a haven for many who have been jaded by the folk culture that seems to be part and parcel of the Canadian evangelical Christian scene. These people often value the Anglican liturgy. The faithful preaching of Scripture week after week is the backbone of the evangelistic work in the parish. Scripture has a powerful but subtle effect on people.

The members of St. John's are professionals, business people, whose office output is expected to be very high indeed. The attitude that "I am in control. I am in charge. There is nothing that we can't do." has always to be recognized and challenged, i.e. "Knowledge (which abounds in the congregation) puffs up (and the bubble can be pricked with a pin), but love (which is in short supply in our society) builds up" (1 Corinthians 8: 1). So we need to keep measuring ourselves as a congregation by John 13:34 and 35. (REM)

The background of many people in the parish has one or a combination of the following:

Mennonite Communalism
They have excelled in university and professional training. Their parents were sustained and kept by Mennonite Christianity which brought them out of Europe or Russia to a new land where they were pioneers and very much strengthened and kept by

their faith. Their children, have gone on to excel in various professions, and have found their Mennonite background, though admirable, of no personal value or significance to them in the world in which they now live.

Pentecostal Emotionalism
The Pentecostal experience, i.e. a highly emotional/experience oriented encounter with the Christian religion, which they had as children, has subsequently failed to grow with them as they mature and their situation changes socially, economically and intellectually and as they mature.

Liberal Anglicanism
Liberal Anglicanism, rather than embracing the Gospel and facing the issues of the day, has taken the stance, "face the issues of the day and determine if the Gospel is relevant".

Anglican Folk Religion.[3]
This maintains church attendance, the aesthetics of Anglican worship – baptism, marriage and funerals – according to the ancient Anglican liturgy with the lessons read preferably in the King James Version. This religion is very comforting in times of stress, but has little relevance to a life in the every-day world.

Baptist Moralism
This produced a morally rigid stance as an expression of having received the Gospel, ending up in the conclusion that the Gospel is much more a matter of behaviour than belief. The moral issues which are of great importance in teens and early twenties are often less important in mature life.

Roman Catholic Traditionalism
This produced a high level of guilt in people and made categorical demands on them. People broke away from it by reason of failing to observe the requirements. The whole authoritarian tradition of Romanism seems to demand a submission that people are unwilling to make.

Christian Science and Unitarianism
The absolutes of Science robbed many people of Gospel faith who still maintained nominal membership in the Church. They

were benevolent agnostics still adhering to Anglican folk religion, but believing the only truth was scientific.

In many people, the soil of their hearts has been burnt over by these various spiritual brush fires and the good soil has become shallow, rocky and full of weeds. An enormous amount of help is required for the Gospel to get rooted in the soil of the hearts of people who have experienced one or a combination of these fires.

Forest fires occur naturally and burn off old growth and too dense underbush so that a new forest can grow. It is said that in order for the seed of the Douglas Fir Tree to germinate, the seed requires ground that has been burnt over. So, in some instances the forest fires devastate the ground and make growth impossible, while in other they clear the ground for new growth. The fires I've spoken of above are the kind of fires which clear away a too-dense undergrowth and make it possible for new forests to grow.

In contrast to these, the fire of modern secularism has done a lot of damage to the soil. In either case, it is essential that the seed which is the Word of God which contains the Gospel of Jesus Christ in its fullness has got to be confronted by people, not in terms of the traditions in which it has been enshrined for (sometimes) centuries, nor necessarily in institutions in which it has been privatized, but as the autonomous truth in which the purpose of God, the purpose of man, and the purpose of history are contained.[4]

A young couple exemplify much of what I have tried to describe. The wife, "Elizabeth", was brought up on the Eastern Seaboard of the United States as a Roman Catholic. She went to private school, graduated, went to the best university on the West Coast and abandoned her Roman Catholicism which was the religion of her family. She was deeply impressed by the study of English literature, but not to the point where in it she either discovered or was able to articulate personal faith in Jesus Christ. She is now the mother of a small boy. In accordance with the tradition of her family, it is very important that this boy should be baptized to provide a comfort zone for the family against the child's vulnerability to the shortness and uncertainty of human life. The supposition is that as an adult, he will choose for himself what his faith may or may not be, but as a child he should be brought under at least the family covenant with God.

"Elizabeth" is married to a very bright young professional in the first years of a career that will, in all probability, lead to distinction and preferment. He himself was brought up in what was once an Anglican school. At 14, he discovered the amazing hypocrisy, as he understood it, of those who drank heavily on Saturday night and prayed earnestly on Sunday morning. He formally abandoned the Church after having been in the choir, a server and after having served in all sorts of other capacities in the Church. He distinguished himself at university, went on to graduate studies where again he distinguished himself and qualified in his profession. He is very idealistic with regard to the nature of the family and the moral constraints within which one must conduct business in his contemporary secular world. He is convinced that the great values that undergird our society are those that are generally identified as Christian. He lives with the conviction that in the crucible of history, those Christian values have withstood the test as no other system has. But one of the absolute points of personal conviction is that he is not prepared under any circumstances to confess a personal faith in God the Father, God the Son and God the Holy Spirit as would be required if he were to bring his child for baptism to the Church.

The work of evangelism is marked by this kind of burnt-over ground. The Church as an institution is discounted and tradition is respected for its significance in shaping a culture, but has no intrinsic worth in terms of the values it maintains. The future belongs to those who will not bow the knee to anyone, nor confess the name of anyone outside of themselves. This is what I mean by "evangelism in burnt-over country."

How Evangelism Works

Nevertheless, the Church as an institution provides at least a beach-head in the community for the work of evangelism. Respect for traditions without dependence upon them provides a setting in which a dialectic can take place. Worship honest and sincere helps people to articulate the affirmations they feel and the questions that haunt them. It allows them to acknowledge in an ordered way something of the spiritual reality that they can't escape. It also provides a *proto evangelium*. It also provides the opportunity for both the reading and the preaching of Scripture on a regular basis. This then forms the community matrix in which the work of evangelism and discipling takes place. It creates a central community from which small groups for Bible study, prayer and fellowship spin off. This is turn creates a context for mutual pastoral concern, evangelistic concern and for the bonds of Christian fellowship to be strengthened. When, in the parish, a special effort in evangelism is required, homes are opened for dessert parties, downtown business lunches and gatherings for women at the local golf and country club take place. A good deal of personal evangelism between individuals also goes on.

The personal giftedness and leadership from individual members of the congregation of a wide variety of social, economic, intellectual and spiritual backgrounds, provides some very strong Christian hybrids who bring to their membership in the Anglican Church at least some of the treasures of their background in other churches. They seem to have more endurance qualities in our contemporary secular world and will form a considerable resource for Christian growth in the next 50 years.

Footnotes.

1. See Michael Nazir-Ali "A servant of the servants of God" *CMS Newsletter* No. 492 January/February 1990 (CMS, Partnership House, 157 Waterloo Road, London SE1 8UU)

2. See Stephen Neill *Anglicanism* (Harmondsworth, Pelican) and J. I. Packer *The Evangelical Anglican Identity Problem* (Latimer Studies, 1, 131 Banbury Road, Oxford)

3. "Folk Religion with a Christian veneer . . . the possibility of using such folk religion as a bridge to bring people to greater commitment and understanding." *CMS Newsletter*, January/February 1990, p 2.

4. See Acts 17 and Paul's sermon to the Athenians; *The Great Code* by Northrop Frye; Lesslie Newbigin's *Foolishness to the Greeks* (London, S.P.C.K., 1986).

Chapter Fifteen

The U.S.A: Evangelism among Jewish People

Simcha Newton

Introduction

"Brethren, my heart's desire and my prayer to God for Israel is that they may be saved." Romans 10:1

I too can echo that prayer with Paul. I was born and raised in a Jewish home. I came to believe in Jesus as my Messiah, and like Paul, the Lord has given me the desire to see my own people come to know Jesus personally. Since becoming a Christian, I have been privileged to be associated with two different Jewish mission organizations: Jews For Jesus (JFJ) and A Christian Ministry among Jewish People (CMJ).

A Christian Ministry among Jewish People is the official name of CMJ/USA. They have three stated purposes: first, to encourage Jewish people to recognize Jesus as their Messiah; second, to educate Christians, especially Episcopalians, about the Jewish origins of our Faith; and third, to encourage and support Jewish believers as well as to foster relationships between Jewish and Gentile believers in Jesus. The central focus is that Jewish people will be saved. Jewish evangelism occurs both through the direct ministry of CMJ/USA and indirectly through those that CMJ/USA has educated and equipped to evangelize.

In this Decade of Evangelism, it is important that we not only remember to bring the Gospel to the Jewish people, but also that we see Jewish evangelism as part of God's total strategy for world evangelization. Two comments seem relevant at this point. First, Paul, even as the missionary to the Gentiles, set a pattern of going to his own people first (Acts 13:4,5; 14:1, 16:11–13; 17:1–2,10,16–17; 18:1–4; 19:1,8; 28:16–17). Second, in Romans 1:16, Paul states that the Gospel is "to the Jew first and then to the Gentile". The good news of Jesus is for everyone, but there is a priority. A good explanation was given by the Lausanne Committee for Jewish Evangelism in their report from 1980:

> There is, therefore a great responsibility laid upon the Church to share Christ with the Jewish people. This is not to imply that Jewish evangelism is more important in the sight of God, or that those involved in Jewish evangelism have a higher calling. We observe that the practical application of the scriptural priority is difficult to understand and apply. We do not suggest that there should be a radical application of 'to the Jew first' in calling on all the evangelists, missionaries, and Christians to seek out the Jews within their sphere of witness before speaking to non-Jews! Yet we do call the Church to restore ministry among the covenanted people of God to its biblical place in its strategy of world evangelization.[1]

Remember that Jews are part of the Great Commission; not as part of the Great Omission. David Harley reported, "It is said that Charles Simeon was waxing eloquent at a meeting once, talking about the need of the six million Jews of the world to hear the Gospel, when someone pointed out that there were six hundred million non-Jews in equal need. To which Simeon is reported to have replied: 'What if the six million are, in God's strategy, the key to reach the six hundred million? What then?' "[2]

Sadly, in the Episcopal Church USA, many of our most heated battles are fought for the right even to do Jewish evangelism. For example, in The Episcopalian, February 1990, there was a full page article entitled "Evangelizing Jews should not be a part of the 'Decade'". Additionally, in a recent devotional guide published by the Episcopal Church, an issue is devoted to Jewish–Christian dialogue. In it they "... offer meditations which are sensitive to a more gentle theological *pluralism* [italics mine]". The theology behind this viewpoint will be discussed under the section on Resistance.

Context

Who are these people that we have come to know as the Jews? According to Jewish Orthodox law, one is Jewish if born from a

Jewish mother. In modern usage, the definition would be expanded to include one with any Jewish parentage or one who has converted to Judaism and is not a member of a different faith.

The Israeli Supreme Court has issued a recent ruling that Jews who believe in Jesus *do not* qualify as Jews for the Law of Return. The Law of Return states that "every Jew has a right to come to this country (Israel) as an *oleh* (immigrant)". The ruling says that for this purpose a person who is baptized a Christian is a member of a different faith. However, atheistic Jews still qualify.

Jewish people live throughout the world, with the majority in the United States, Israel, and Russia.[3] Different Jewish communities will manifest a wide variance of beliefs and customs. Although most of these individuals exhibit a strong sense of Jewish identity "I was born a Jew and I'll die a Jew", assimilation has become an erosive factor.

An important component that has influenced the Jewish community against the Gospel has been the Church herself. The Church does not have a strong positive history when dealing with the Jews.

One only has to look at the Inquisition, the Crusades, the Russian Pogroms. The Holocaust, for the Jew, would also be added to that list. In their thinking, the Holocaust is seen as a Christian massacre, as the culmination of Christian persecution throughout the centuries. The Jews remember that Hitler was a baptized Christian and that the Church did not stand up to the holocaust. While there was much openness among Jews to Christian faith before World War Two, evangelism is now seen as an extension of the holocaust.[4] The wounds between the Church and the Jewish people are deep and must not be treated superficially. Throughout history as the church has attempted to relate to Jewish people there have been factors which have prevented the Jews from being receptive to the Gospel. For instance, being labeled as "Christ killers"; church language that is full of jargon and emotionally laden, i.e., "washed in the blood of the lamb" or "convert"; then also hearing all of one's life that Jews cannot believe in Jesus; and finally compounded by the Church's teaching that once one believes, one is no longer Jewish. Unfortunately, the list of the Church's insensitivities goes on.

History

My interest in Jewish evangelism grew slowly. At first I just wanted to be a good Christian. Being Jewish was not really a part of it, or so I thought. My Gentile Christian friends, however, kept coming to me and asking for information on how to witness to their Jewish friends.

As I began to develop more of a burden for Jewish evangelism, I became involved as a volunteer with Jews For Jesus (JFJ). As a result, they asked me to move to San Francisco to take part in their missionary training programme. That was not in the career path I had planned, for I was an auditor with the Department of the Inspector General for the federal Department of Agriculture. However, the Lord made it clear that it was indeed his plan. Through JFJ's training program, I not only learned a lot about evangelism and basic Christian doctrine, but also a lot about my own unique Jewish heritage and background. As a result of the training and association with other Jewish believers, my identity as a *Jewish* believer became more evident in my life.

After the training period, Jews For Jesus chose to use my administrative skills rather than my evangelistic ones and I became the manager of their accounting department. Nevertheless, I was still involved in the ongoing work of the ministry.

My involvement with CMJ/USA came after I married Peter Newton, an Episcopalian in 1986. We came to Trinity Episcopal School for Ministry in 1988 so that Peter could prepare for ordination. While at seminary, I was excited to learn that the Episcopal Church had an active outreach to Jewish people. I have become a volunteer with CMJ/USA as a diocesan representative and now as a field missionary. I am looking forward to a more direct involvement with CMJ/USA in the future.

CMJ was founded in 1809 as The London Society for Promoting Christianity among the Jews. It was nicknamed the London Jew's Society (LJS). It is, as far as we know, the oldest Jewish missionary society in the world today. Joseph Frey, son of a rabbi in Berlin, became a Christian in the 1780's. He became a missionary with the London Missionary Society that began in 1799. In 1809 a decision was made to create a separate organization to minister to the Jewish population, hence LJS was born. Within 40 years, LJS had founded mission stations to the Jews in such diverse places as Warsaw, Jerusalem, Smyrna,

Bucharest, and Cairo. By 1914, there were workers on four continents. Evangelistic work was being done by LJS in England, Austria, Romania, Syria, Egypt, Tunis, Israel, and Canada. After World War II, LJS changed its name to the Church's Ministry among the Jews (CMJ/UK).

The work began in the United States in 1816 when Joseph Frey moved to New York. He was associated with LJS until 1842. Between 1842 and 1878 there were small outreaches by individual Episcopalians. However in 1878 the Episcopal Church formed "the Church Society for Promoting Christianity Amongst the Jews" (clearly viewing itself as the North American branch of the Anglican Society). The Episcopal Church was the only denomination whose governing body had an organized effort for Jewish evangelism between 1878 and 1882. There were 32 bishops on the Board. The society operated until 1904. During those years the Society had missions and schools in many places including: New York, Philadelphia, New Orleans and Baltimore. However, these centres closed down in 1904 due to a lack of funds. The final report of the society cites it was closed because ". . . impossible to overcome the prevailing condition of apathy . . ." within the church.[5] There was no organized work in the United States by Episcopalians after that until 1982 when CMJ/USA set up its headquarters in Fairfax, VA. CMJ/USA is now moving to Ambridge, PA to make use of the training facilities of Trinity Episcopal School for Ministry and the new Stanway Institute of World Missions and Evangelism.

Indicators

Indicators that CMJ/USA is having an effect upon the Church as well as upon the Jewish community can be seen both positively and negatively. On the positive side, we can anticipate an increase in supporters both congregationally and individually, the number of preachments, and the number of field missionaries. Field missionaries are people around the country with a heart for Jewish evangelism. They volunteer to give several hours a month to CMJ/USA and build prayer support, speak in churches, represent CMJ/USA at diocesan events, and generally assist CMJ/USA to the end that Jewish people will be saved. The number of new Jewish believers is not an indicator of CMJ/

USA's efforts because much of the missionary work is primarily done through the local parish. CMJ/USA equips and enables lay people to do the actual witnessing. Many Jewish people have been reached through the fruit of CMJ/USA's teaching ministry.

There are also negative indicators that enable CMJ/USA to gauge some of its effectiveness. Often those who do not agree can be vocal in their opposition. One example was the election of the last presiding bishop. There was much negative media attention given to two of the four finalists, The Rt. Rev. William C. Frey, then Bishop of Colorado and Rt. Rev. Furman Stough, then Bishop of Alabama, because they were on CMJ/USA's Board of Advisors. Some would say that it cost them the election. They both remain supportive and Bishop Frey is still on the Board of Advisors.

Method

Historically, in both England and the United States, the major method of evangelism was to provide social services for the new immigrant communities. In England, CMJ/UK had a complex of buildings in London known as Palestine Place. A church was opened in 1814 that was the first place of worship specifically for Jewish believers. This complex housed a missionary college and schools for both boys and girls. Having their own printing press, they taught unemployed Jewish believers the trades of printing and book–binding. In 1817 CMJ/UK first published a Hebrew New Testament. In the United States, CMJ had private schools for Jewish boys and girls associated with their missions. The material needs of the Jewish community are no longer paramount. Now the Jews have one overriding need: they need to know Jesus.

There are several different methods of evangelism that CMJ/USA is currently using. Most are ministries within the Church to equip the members to be able to share the Gospel with those Jewish people with whom they may be in contact. CMJ/USA sponsors Jewish Evangelism Seminars, circulates literature, holds Passover demonstrations, and presents other seminars on the Jewish roots of the faith.

Recent surveys have shown that most Jewish people have come to believe in Jesus primarily through the witness of a Gentile

Christian friend. Missionaries or trained lay people are helpful at
three times in the process. In the beginning, the trained person
proclaims that Jews can and do believe in Jesus; allowing the
friend to follow up. In the middle, the friend has talked to the
Jewish inquirer about the Lord. The friend can then refer this
inquirer to a trained person to do in–depth Bible study and
answer questions. Finally, the inquirer may just need to meet
someone who actually is Jewish and believes in Jesus or who
knows how to bring an inquirer to a point of decision.

Jews For Jesus (JFJ) has taken radical steps in the field of
Jewish evangelism with their literature and bold witness. As their
literature implies, JFJ believes in lifting up the name of Jesus, as
well as sowing abundant seed through their tract distribution.
JFJ has produced unique materials that would appeal to a Jewish
audience. Tracts, media advertisements, books, evangelistic
campaigns are only some of their methods. Their tracts are easy
to read, with intriguing titles like "Jesus made me Kosher" and
"Christmas is a Jewish Holiday". Each year, during the Advent
season, JFJ has placed advertisements in major newspapers and
publications, such as *The New York Times* and *TIME* magazine.
These advertisements proclaim the Gospel in a Jewish way and
offer a book or cassette tape for more information. Through
these methods, most people become aware, especially in the
Jewish community, that there are Jews who do believe in Jesus.
However, most of the work of Jews for Jesus is personal. The
missionaries meet with Jewish people who are interested in
knowing more about Jesus and explore the scriptures, one to
one.

Message

The focus of the message to the Jew must centre on the Good
News that Jesus is the Messiah promised by the prophets. Jesus
is Jewish, the Apostles are Jewish, all the writers of the Bible are
Jewish, with the possible exception of Luke. Believing in Jesus
does not make one a Gentile; in fact, if Jesus is the Messiah, then
the most Jewish thing one can do, is to believe in the Jewish
Messiah.

The Old Testament Scriptures pave the way for a Jew to
accept Jesus. Since these writings point to a predicted Messiah, it
can be shown that Jesus was the fulfilment of those prophecies.

Glimpses of the Christian doctrine of the Trinity also can be seen in the Old Testament and provide a foundation to demonstrate that we do not believe in three gods, but in the one true God of Abraham, Isaac, and Jacob. The Gospel of Matthew is especially helpful in showing how the teachings of Jesus are the fulfilment of the Law and the prophets.

The centre of the discussion during evangelism must focus on, "Who is Jesus?". It is too easy to become entangled in side issues and tangents such as the history of the Church and the Holocaust. These tangents are mostly ploys to avoid dealing with the real problem: Is Jesus the Messiah, the Son of the living God? And if so, what does that now require of me?

Effect

The effects of CMJ/USA's ministry can be seen upon individuals and upon the Episcopal Church. CMJ/USA is represented on the Presiding Bishop's Committee on Jewish–Christian Relations. When this group developed "Guidelines for Christian–Jewish Relations" at the 1988 General Convention, CMJ/USA had input regarding the section entitled "Authentic Christian Witness". They were successful in having "among all peoples" added to the end of the sentence: "Christians see that same God embodied in the person of Jesus Christ, to whom the Church must bear witness by word and deed among all peoples." CMJ/USA also attempted to have "uniquely" inserted between "God" and "embodied", but unfortunately was unsuccessful.

The impact of Jewish evangelism upon individuals varies between Jews and Gentiles. Gentiles, as one supporter said, begin to understand perhaps for the first time the Jewish roots of their faith. Speaking about a seminar on "How to Introduce Your Jewish Friends to Jesus" the supporter went on to say, "It has also given me a greater love and appreciation of the Jewishness of our Messiah, of the Jewish roots of our faith, and of the Jewish context within which the Scriptures were written."

Jewish believers within the Episcopal church are encouraged and supported by knowing that there are other Jewish believers. A deacon wrote to us: "Thanks to you and your CMJ/USA presentation, January 1990 marks a turning point in my life as a Jewish Christian. What had formerly been presented as a handicap, was presented as wholeness. What had been a source of sadness over leaving something behind, was the joy of having found and having been found by it. What had been covered over as useless, was given back as a gift. Thank you, thank you, thank you from my heart."

Jewish believers and others are appreciative of the tools they are given to share the Gospel with the Jewish people in their lives. A Jewish believer who is the wife of a priest said concerning CMJ/USA: "My own church did not have the tools necessary to teach me to minister to my own family! I met Father Bottomley through the ministry of CMJ, and was finally given tools to begin approaching my family with the Gospel in a way not alien or hostile."

Jewish evangelism also has an effect upon other members of the Church. Gentile believers are strengthened in their own faith when they see that Jewish people are coming to the Lord. Could the Jews coming to faith signal another step in God's prophetic plan? As Paul says, "Now I am speaking to you Gentiles . . . For if their [the Jews'] rejection means reconciliation of the world, what will their acceptance mean, but life from the dead?" (Romans 11:13–15).

Discipleship and the Church

CMJ/USA has not been involved with planting churches nor is this part of its strategy. Although there are some other Jewish missions that have planted congregations. At present there are 50 to 60 Messianic congregations in the United States. Most of the congregations are small, independent and not affiliated with a major denomination. However, the congregations have begun to organize themselves. Messianic congregations at present can affiliate with one of three organized groups: Union of Messianic Congregations (UJMC), the Messianic Jewish Alliance of America (MJAA), and the Fellowship of Messianic Congregation (FMC). The congregations vary greatly in style and format. Some follow a basic church format with a Jewish flavour while others follow mostly a synagogue liturgical style which would include New Testament readings and sermons about Y'shua (Hebrew for Jesus).

Resistance

Strong resistance to Jewish evangelism comes from all sides and in many forms. Most obvious is the opposition from the Jewish community itself, which perceives evangelism as a new "Holocaust", that is bent on taking away their very fibre and being. They view evangelism as an atrocity just as hideous as those committed by the Nazis and provoke vigorous comments: "Hasn't the Church already done enough harm?" or "You cannot be Jewish and believe in Jesus. It is like a dog becoming a cat."

One method of dealing with this resistance within the Jewish community is to see it as a barometer of the effectiveness of Jewish evangelism. If the Jewish community is not responding and no one is being reached for the Lord, is our evangelism having any effect? Response to that question does not give us a license to witness insensitively or to provoke needlessly. When the Jewish community responds negatively, perhaps the truth of our message is indeed being heard. Just as the Apostle Paul displayed a fierce opposition before he came to faith, so too we may see some of our strongest critics become believers. "For I can testify about them that they are zealous for God, but their zeal is not based on knowledge" (Romans 10:2).

We also find resistance from within the Church. This is the case for CMJ/USA. Sadly, to date, more effort has been spent fighting battles within the Episcopal Church than doing active evangelism. There are three main groups within the universal Church that oppose Jewish evangelism. These groups can be categorized by how they view the relationship between Israel and the Church.

Israel above the Church
The first group sees Israel above the Church. They are sometimes referred to as those who "Bless Israel". They are evangelicals who wholeheartly support Israel because of their eschatology. Their view towards Israel spills over into their opinion of evangelism. One organization, the International Christian Embassy, Jerusalem (ICEJ) boasts of their "non–evangelistic witness". They do not try to share their faith unless asked. Byron Spradlin, a member of the Jews For Jesus board comments: "Perhaps they think the Great Commission says 'Go ye into all the world and wait till around till someone asks

you' ".[6] Nevertheless, ICEJ has wide reaching support among evangelicals in Europe, Scandinavia, and North America. Their emphasis is ". . . on 'friendship development' and preoccupation with eschatological speculation can subtly divert Christians from their evangelistic and prophetic responsibilities. In these days when Israeli Jews are increasingly receptive to the gospel, it is tragic that 'Christian Zionists' are withholding from them their greatest treasure: Jesus Christ."[7] Friendship evangelism is not wrong, but this group gives the impression that talking about Jesus and being supportive of Israel do not mix. It is tragic that those who are so supportive of Israel and her future, do not want to take the risk of sharing the good news of Jesus.

Two-covenant theology

The second group is the most active in the Episcopal Church. They see Israel as equal to the church. This is referred to as two-covenant theology. Simply put, there are two ways of salvation. The Jews have salvation through Moses and the Old Covenant, and the Gentiles through Jesus and the New Covenant. Put another way, this theory says that Jesus is the way for Gentiles to come to God, but that Jews are already related to God through the primary or eternal covenant made with the people of Israel. The roots of the two-covenant theology are based on their doctrines of Christ and salvation. Therefore, the result of this thinking is that it is both unnecessary and entirely inappropriate to encourage Jews to become believers in Jesus.

Two major implications have grown out of this two-covenant theology. The first is that the Jews do not need the Gospel because they have their own covenant, which has led towards universalism. The second result has been the growth of the Jewish–Christian dialogue movement. Both have led the Church away from witnessing to Jewish people.

The two-covenant theology is contrary to Scripture, not only in the Old, but also in the New Testament. It implies that the two covenants are parallel, and that Moses and Jesus are equal mediators of their respective covenants. Both of the covenants are made first with Jews (Jeremiah 31:31ff). Indeed the Jews were the first beneficiaries of both covenants. Also Peter, when speaking to his Jewish brethren of the Sanhedrin (Acts 4:12) said, "Neither is there salvation in any other; for there is no other name under heaven given among men, whereby we must be saved." Paul asserts that there is only "one mediator between God and men, the man Christ Jesus, who gave Himself as a ransom for all men" (1 Timothy 2:5–6). Either Jesus is the mediator of the one eternal covenant, the one perfect sacrifice for sins, the Messiah for Jews and Gentiles, or all of us, both Jew and Gentile alike, are excluded from that covenant.

The other ramification of the two-covenant theology is the increase in Jewish/Christian dialogue. Both two-covenant theology and dialogue are from the same liberal world view. The proponents of this theology have been leaders in the dialogue movement. Dialogue is important for there have been many misunderstandings between Jews and Gentiles. It is always good to promote open discussions between groups where there have been misconceptions and inadequate information. Philip Bottomley of CMJ/USA said, "In other words, dialogue is important, but it is not the same thing as that which Christ commands in the Great Commission. While it would be wrong to have a hidden agenda in dialogue, nonetheless, I believe any Christian who does not state as part of his story that Christ claims to be the exclusive way to the Father is being false to his own story and so invalidates the dialogue."

The Abrahamic Accord
The writers of the previously cited article "Evangelizing Jews should not be part of the 'Decade' ", are the founders of the Abrahamic Accord. This organization began in 1985 to facilitate dialogue between Christians and Jews. They state in the article: ". . . this new evangelism calls for a triumphalist vision of Christian conversion. Some of the new evangelists *even* [italics mine] call for the conversion of God's special people, the Jews." The article goes on to say: "Instead of converting the Jews, we should be repenting of those terrible centuries of neglect . . ."[8] If Jesus is the Jewish Messiah, then it is the worst form of anti-Semitism or neglect *not* to tell the Jews about Jesus. Most of the Jewish leaders are excited about the dialogue; they are hoping that it will replace evangelism. Let us not lose our focus on the Great Commission to reach all with the Gospel.

Israel beneath the Church
The last sector of the Church that opposes Jewish evangelism sees Israel as beneath the Church. The core of the teaching is that

the Church is the "New Israel", and because the Jews rejected Jesus, God rejected them as his chosen people, and he took away the kingdom from the Jews and gave it "to a nation producing the fruits of it" (Matthew 21:43). In other words, the Church has replaced Israel. It is justifiable, indeed correct, to talk of the Church as the people of God superseding the Jews. God through Christ has replaced a national people with a people called out from all nations including Israel, but not confined to it.

Any suggestion that God would annul his own covenant with Israel as people and transfer it to others is entirely opposite to the whole tenor of the Bible, the nature of covenant and indeed the nature of God. Certainly, God talks about punishing Israel for their adultery. Nonetheless, the Lord made promises that he would not desert the Jewish people despite all their wickedness (Jeremiah 31:35–37).

Paul deals specifically with the subject of the relation of Israel and the Church in Romans 9–11. He strongly asserts that Israel has not been abandoned by her God, nor replaced by Gentile believers. Paul concludes that Israel will be restored to full potential: "For the gifts and the call of God are irrevocable" (Romans 11:29). The Lord has and will continue his promises to the Jewish people.

The teaching that the Church is the "New Israel" when applied to evangelistic strategy tends to mean that the Jewish people as such have no special significance. Therefore the sense of urgency to evangelize the Jewish people is lost. Those who hold to this teaching do not see any virtue in focusing mission on such a small group as the Jews. Or they find fault with Jewish missions because of our support for the State of Israel which they see without biblical basis, and contrary to a true Christian attitude towards the oppressed Palestinians. As long as the Church, God's "New Israel", is heir to all God's promises, it is not surprising that only the curses are left for the Jews. Followers of this teaching are also susceptible to the anti-missionary lie that one cannot be both a Jew and a Christian. Paul's assertion that ". . . the Gospel is the power of God unto salvation . . . to the Jew first and also to the Greek" (Romans 1:16) is lost on them.

Two-covenant theology adherents are attacking Jewish evangelism from the outside, while those who hold to the "New Israel" teaching are attacking from the inside the evangelical wing. This later teaching can be just as dangerous and far more subtle. Fortunately, CMJ/USA is addressing these theological battles within the Episcopal Church.

To respond to attacks upon the need for Jewish evangelism "The Willowbank Declaration on the Christian Gospel and the Jewish People" was prepared.[9] This statement drafted in April 1989 by several evangelical scholars from around the world was sponsored by World Evangelical Fellowship. In the preamble it states, "This Declaration is made in response to growing doubts and widespread confusion among Christians about the need for, and the propriety of, endeavours to share faith in Jesus with Jewish people." The conclusion declares: "Together, the participants commend this document to the churches with a call to prayerfully consider and act upon these very serious matters as touching the Christian Gospel and the Jewish People." Thanks be to God, there are those in the Church who are willing to take a stand for the need of Jewish evangelism.

Conclusion

Despite the two-edged resistance from within and from without the Church, we need to press forward to include the evangelism of the Jewish people when worldwide evangelism is being discussed.

Two summaries that were written by others focus upon the need for Jewish evangelism. First from the Willowbank Declaration, Article IV.23,

> We affirm that it is unChristian, unloving, and discriminatory, to propose a moratorium on the evangelizing of any part of the human race, and that failure to preach the Gospel to Jewish people would be a form of anti-Semitism, depriving this particular community of its right to hear the Gospel.
>
> We deny that we have sufficient warrant to assume or anticipate the salvation of anyone who is not a believer in Jesus Christ.

Additionally, the conclusion of the Lausanne report, states, "Including Jewish people is a test of our willingness to be involved in world evangelization. It is a test of our faith in the one exclusive way of salvation and our proclamation of Christ as an adequate Saviour for those who are apparently adequate so far as worldly righteousness is concerned."[10]

CMJ, in both the United States and England has consistently stood and practised the principle that: "The Gospel is the power of God for salvation, to everyone who believes, to the Jew first and also to the Greek." (Romans 1:16)

The Collect for the Conversion of Jews (from Canadian Book of Common Prayer, p.41) reads:

> O God, who didst choose Israel to be thine inheritance: Look, we beseech thee, upon thine ancient people; open their hearts that they may see and confess the Lord Jesus to be thy Son and their true Messiah, and, believing, they may have life through his Name. Take away all pride and prejudice in us that may hinder their understanding of the Gospel, and hasten the time when all Israel shall be saved; through the merits of the same Jesus Christ our Lord. Amen.

Resources

Barker, Walter. *A Fountain Opened A short history of the Church's Ministry among the Jews 1809–1982*, (London: Olive Press, 1983)

CMJ/USA, 10523 Main St, Suite 38. Fairfax, VA 22030, USA

CMJ/UK, 30c Clarence Road, St. Albans, Herts, AL1 4JJ, England

Jews For Jesus, 60 Haight St., San Francisco, CA 94102, USA.

Lausanne Occasional Papers. *The Thailand Report: Christian Witness to the Jewish People* (Lausanne Committee on World Evangelization, PO Box 1100, Wheaton, IL 60187, USA). A report of the mini–consultation on reaching Jewish people from conference held in Pattaya, Thailand 1980. Excellent report on the major aspects of Jewish evangelism.

Lausanne Consultation on Jewish Evangelism, Ellebaekvey 5, DK8520, Lystrup, Denmark. They publish a quarterly magazine, discussing current topics in Jewish evangelism.

Meldau, Fred John. *Messiah in Both Testaments* (Christian Victory Publishing Company, 1967). Presents messianic prophecies that demonstrate that Jesus is the only one who could have fulfilled them.

Rosen, Moishe and Ceil. *Share the New Life With a Jew* (Chicago: Moody Press, 1976). Clear, concise information geared towards lay people on how to witness to the Jewish people in their life.

Willowbank Declaration on the Christian Gospel and the Jewish People. 1989. Theological statement to affirm the need for and the appropriateness of witnessing to Jewish people. Sponsored by World Evangelical Fellowship, Wheaton, IL.

World Christian (Summer 1989). The whole issue is devoted to mission to the Jewish people. Four main areas are covered: The Holocaust, the State of Israel, the Hebrew Christians, and the Mission.

Footnotes

1. Lausanne Occasional Paper 7, Thailand Report, "Christian Witness to the Jewish People", 1980, p.5.
2. David Harley, "Bible College and Seminaries: Vanguards in Missions", Paper presented as part of the Jewish Evangelism track at Lausanne II in Manila, July 1989.
3. The percentage figures of the World Jewish Population are as follows: North America 44.6%, Europe 7.9%, USSR 16.9%, Africa 1.3%, South Asia 23.1%, Oceania .5%, East Asia .009%. The ten largest Jewish Communities are United States 5,920,890; Israel 3,436,100; USSR 2,630,000; France 650,000; United Kingdom 410,000; Canada 305,000; Argentina 300,000; Brazil 150,000; South Africa 118,000; Hungary 80,000. The total world population of Jews is 18.2 million.
4. Ron Gitelman, "Jewish Evangelism Before and After the Holocaust" in *World Christian*, June 1989, p.77.
5. Bob Mendelsohn, unpublished paper "The Rise and Fall of Evangelism of the Jews by the Episcopal Church in the United States", Summer, 1988, p.4.
6. Byron Spradlin, "Sapping the Strength of Witness in Israel", *Evangelical Missions Quarterly*, January 1985, p.24–28.
7. "The State of Israel", *World Christian*, Summer 1989, p.30.
8. George Hunt, J. Daniel Burke, and James Lassen-Williams, "Evangelizing Jews should not be a part of the 'Decade' ", *The Episcopalian*, February, 1990, p.27.
9. Lausanne Occasional Paper 7, Thailand Report, "Christian Witness to the Jewish People", 1980.
10. op.cit: p.21.

Chapter Sixteen

Australia: Evangelism among Businessmen and Decision-Makers

Alan Nichols

Context

Melbourne is a highly suburban city of 3,000,000 people with development corridors of new commercial housing, mixed with public housing. One third of Melbourne's residents were born overseas, or are the children of those born overseas. There are large populations of Greeks, Italians and more recently Vietnamese. They tend to congregate in ethnic enclaves. Church-going in this very secular nation is at about 20% of the population, but high Catholic and Orthodox attendances obscure low Protestant success in evangelism, or even in handing on the faith to our own children.

Although "post-Christian" like England, and highly commercial and materialistic like the United States, Australians nevertheless have underlying values of mateship, egalitarianism and concern for the underdog, reflected in a comprehensive social security system and high government commitment to welfare programmes.

Most social research indicates that the decline in church-going has been arrested, but that Protestant church-goers have an average age of around 55 years. Therefore the churches have little future unless they engage in effective evangelism among the young.

History

All Churches have evangelistic programmes of some kind, but a lot of it is in fact catechism of the children of regular church-goers. Churches are becoming conscious that they need to work on the very poor and the very rich. The Anglican Diocese of Melbourne has an Evangelism Department, using local and international evangelism programmes, with about half the 240 parishes of the Diocese showing interest. The Diocese also has a Multicultural Ministry Department which has developed 22 ethnic congregations, some of whom have paid ministry, among Vietnamese, Maoris, Persians, Sri Lankans, Spanish-speakers, and others.

My own involvement in evangelism in the city has not been through the official Department of Evangelism, but based on twelve years of church leadership in two roles: Executive Director of the Mission of St James and St John (a family welfare agency attached to a city church) and as Archdeacon of Melbourne (a pastoral role for 46 parishes, working with Regional Bishops) and a Social Responsibility role (as a church spokesperson, and as Chairman of the Diocesan Social Responsibilities Committee).

Over the twelve years, opportunities of personal relations, public policy debates and involvement in Government and Institutional Boards have led to both formal and informal evangelism. Sometimes this has been in the name of the Church, and at other times quite personal. Of whichever kind, these opportunities for social responsibility involvement and for evangelism are now written into my job description as Archdeacon of Melbourne, and so, in that sense, are recognised by the Church. In the areas of social responsibility, my work is assisted by a part-time Project Officer of the Social Responsibilities Committee, and in the areas of evangelism, there is frequent consultation with the Diocesan Department and occasional involvement in their programmes, such as a recent consultancy with the Diocese of Bendigo (a provincial city) looking at new strategies for Mission and Ministry in the parishes of that city. A good deal of this development has been with the support of the late Archbishop, David Penman, on whose staff I worked from July 1986 until his death in October 1989. His public gifts dramatically increased awareness among the general public and in Government and other decision-making circles of the relevance of the Christian Faith to society as a whole and to particular issues as they arose. Within this climate of greater awareness and a positive response from the Church to current issues, evangelism became a more acceptable expression of the Church's confidence in its own message.

Indicators

One would not want to exaggerate the difficulty of individuals in a highly commercial and very secular city turning from agnosticism or atheism towards the Living God. It happens individual by individual, and sometimes as people's general church connection turns into a dynamic personal faith, rather than through identifiable mass movements.

But what can be traced is an acceptance by many city and government leaders that Christian values can be stated overtly as an acceptable basis for thinking through social responsibility, values for the Australian community, and as a basis for peace and justice in the community. The work of the Church in these areas, of course, provides credibility for the value statements. So do relationships between church leaders and other civic leaders. But, as the recent report of the National Committee on Violence has indicated, the clear statement of Christian values about peace and non-violence, based on the character of God as revealed through Jesus Christ, has become not only an acceptable but a praiseworthy statement of how a community can think.

With some very wealthy businessmen, there have been identifiable changes in attitudes and behaviour, particularly in connection with ethics in business decisions and with devoting more time to the family. This marks these Christian men out from their contemporaries, and serves both as a rebuke to greed and a model of better behaviour. These people also give generously to Christian and other charitable causes in a way that is distinctively different from their peers who put everything back into reinvestment for their own personal gain.

Methods

Over twelve years four different methods have been followed: direct verbal evangelism by a church leader to gathered groups of business leaders; taking more seriously politicians and their links with public policy; direct involvement in decision-making bodies on the basis of making a Christian ethical contribution; and discipleship of individual business people.

Challenging Businessmen

The following extract from "Where the River Flows" by Peter and Sue Kaldor explains one particular kind of outreach.

"The view from the central windows of the dining room reached out for kilometres. In front spread the entire city, the lights just coming on in the streets and buildings. The peak hour was nearly over, yet the thousands of moving headlights indicated that the city was still very much alive.

In the foyer people were gathering, exchanging greetings as they sipped a range of drinks provided by the waiters. The host and his wife were welcoming new arrivals.

The scene could have been in the chairman's suite of one of Australia's major companies. It might also have been in one of the more prestigious clubs in the city.

The guests were invited to move into the dining room. Seated around the solid tables, their host stood up and welcomed everybody: 'Thank you for coming tonight. We are gathered to meet with and listen to our most esteemed guest as he shares with us about faith and ethics in the business world. But first I hope you will enjoy your meal.'

The event was one of two meetings aimed at raising Christian consciousness among Australia's senior businessmen. The meetings were planned and executed by senior businessmen themselves, using a church leader of world renown. Similar gatherings were held by lawyers and parliamentarians.

This gathering had been planned for nearly two years. Thirty-two businessmen and their wives were invited, sixteen couples with active Christian involvement and sixteen without such connections. Six months earlier, their secretaries had been rung and asked to keep the date free in their diaries. Then followed an invitation.

The meal was of first-class standard and conversation was flowing. The seating arrangements had been made with a view to bringing people with common interests together. A man with an enthusiasm for the Missionary Aviation Fellowship was seated with the General Manager of a leading Australian airline. While dinner was proceeding, the guest speaker and his wife moved around the tables meeting all the guests.

With dinner completed, coffee and port were served in the lounge as the guest of honour rose to speak. His message was clear and forthright: for sound development, the world needs stability; for stability, we need an ethical framework; and an ethical framework requires faith to endure. A great deal of time was allowed for questions and discussions. At the end, the speaker said he would be happy to talk with anybody individually at any time. Such an opportunity was taken up by several people in the following weeks.

After the event, the host sent all the guests a follow-up letter thanking them for their involvement. A copy of a book written by the guest of honour was included with the letter, along with an offer to talk with the host about any issues that had been raised. In fact, four people took up the offer and he met with them when they had time available. Coincidentally, all four meetings took place in their spare time on business trips – in London!

The world of big business presents an example of a highly specialised sub-culture, within which the communication of faith is best carried out by peers. There is a range of ministries among businessmen, often carried out by informal networks of Christians. Also in Australia there are equivalents of the presidential prayer breakfasts so famous in the United States."

Relationships and Research in Social Responsibility

Archbishop David Penman and I shared a strategy of developing personal relationships with politicians and taking more seriously Christian contributions to social responsibility and the development of public policy. We followed, over five years, a strategy of inviting leading politicians of all Parties to dinners at Bishopscourt and sometimes at other locations in order to establish or develop personal relationships. This gave rise to pastoral opportunities, but also to some direct evangelism with key people in the community.

Behind this was an increased level of seriousness in the Church's social responsibility work, targeting public policy issues which were closest to the nature of the Gospel; for example, dealing with violence and conflict, arising from two dreadful incidents in the streets of Melbourne where deranged people shot wildly and indiscriminately and killed a number of people. This research articulating Christian values, based on Jesus the Peacemaker, was articulated in the published report "Violence and Conflict Resolution".[2] Such contributions gave substance to conversations with politicians and other civic leaders. Because the Christian values were clearly articulated, we had the opportunity of talking about the character of God as revealed in Christ as the basis of those values. Over five years, twelve such dinners were held at Bishopscourt, Melbourne, with twelve or fourteen guests at each. The 'guest of honour' was invited to speak about the issues they faced in their political leadership, and the other guests were invited to comment and discuss. In all cases, personal relationships developed from that point with the political leaders, and led to further opportunities of discussing the relevance of Faith to their world. In one or two cases it meant encouraging a quiet Christian to be more overt; in other cases, it was a matter of commending the Faith to someone with no background of religion at all.

The social responsibility work was a very important back-up to this, as it is so often the content of the debates which politicians hold. So hard work and research, together with articulation of Christian values, provided the basis for much discussion with political leadership. A team of volunteers, plus the part-time Project Officer from the Social Responsibilities Committee, were a very important back-up to developing positions on particular social responsibility matters. Current agenda items for that group in 1990 are:

* Legislation for In Vitro Fertilization;
* Domestic Violence;
* Community Options for Living for Disabled People;
* Justice in Industrial Matters;
* Implications of Social Planning of Cities for Poor People;
* Use of Violence in Law Enforcement.

Involvement in Decision-making Bodies

In a metropolitan city like Melbourne many decisions about the life of the community are made by institutions: State Government, Local Government, hospitals, universities, trade unions, professional associations, and churches and clubs.

On the whole individuals work through these groups and are spokespersons for these groups in terms of public debate. Even State Government sounds out community opinion by 'flying kites' on particular questions before making decisions. In this process there are two opportunities for Christians: as individuals working within those decision-making bodies, or as Church spokespersons commenting in advance or after decisions are made.

Increasingly I believe that Christians, whether Church representatives or Public Servants or community people, need to participate in these decision-making bodies so that their contribution can be positive rather than reactive. I serve, myself, as a Government appointee on the Board of the Royal Victorian Eye and Ear Hospital, and am Chairman of the Ethics and Research Committee of that Hospital; I serve on the Ethics Committee of Austin Hospital, one of many institutional ethics committees throughout Australia making decisions on the ethics of clinical work, research on human beings, and hospital practice. I am on two State Government committees: The Community Council Against Violence (which has been looking into violence in nightclubs and is now looking at domestic violence and how to prevent it) and the Social Justice Consultative Council which advises the Premier on how Social Justice principles of access, equity and participation can be brought into the operations of government at every level. I also write, as an individual, on ethical questions in the Australian Financial Review (a national daily paper for the business sector) and for the Sunday Age (a Melbourne weekly for the educated). These columns are on such topics as Australia's commitment to refugees; integrity among people holding public office; discrimination against women in the work force; effects of economic decisions on local communities; caring for the aged in an ageing population etc.

Such participation and such writing can only be claimed to be 'pre-evangelistic'. But unless Christians are in this arena, how can they ever find opportunities for face to face contact with people who are outside the Church? Local churches have become so busy in their internal committee systems (committees for worship, pastoral care, etc) that people are now becoming aware that they are losing touch with the communities where they work and live. This kind of participation is long-term and arduous, and can only be done by those who have a genuine interest in social responsibility and in pushing the frontiers of the Kingdom of God out into the community. It is quite distinct from, but can be complementary to, direct evangelism through parish missions or through media. They are, in my view, superior to both of those methods, because they bring people into constant face to face contact with people from other religions and no religion. So they are 'in a sense' a better test of obedience to the Lordship of Christ, and when people are converted, it is on the basis of the relevance of faith to everyday life situations.

Discipleship of Individual Business People

At the Lausanne II Congress in the Philippines in July 1989, I conducted a workshop in the Discipleship stream on "Discipleship of Business People". I shared some of our Australian experiences, and found similar experiences from the United States and England. Making friends of individual people in the business sector and being available for pastoral care when things go wrong in their lives, can definitely lead to evangelistic opportunity and then to personal discipleship.

A friend who is a millionaire in business has gone from formal church connection in ten years to making decisions not to support important changes in the company structure for ethical reasons and has suffered as a consequence. The company of which he has been Chairman is now being sold off to provide assets for the rest of the company and his own position phased down. This is a direct consequence of Christian ethics arising from a renewed faith.

Such situations are occurring, I understand from the Lausanne Congress, all over the world where business people in positions of high responsibility within companies face difficult decisions about taxation evasion, company restructuring, retrenchment of loyal staff, closing of offices and factories in areas where the community would deteriorate, and ruthless competition. These are the frontier questions for Christian disciples in business at a high level and when they get personal and pastoral support they are able to make the difficult decisions even to their own disadvantage. But many are not served by their pastors or churches in this area and flounder when the ethical decision is before them. Discipleship of such people has to be 'on the run', grabbing opportunities for dinner, coffee late at night, quick telephone calls around the world, and any other opportunity of keeping in contact and giving support.

At a different level of management, it is possible to have regular Bible studies on Christian ethics in business on a weekly or fortnightly basis. I conducted such a series several years ago in a parish with a high proportion of management people. They expressed great appreciation for providing a framework in which ethical decisions are made, rather than giving black and white 'yes' and 'no' answers to particular questions. It is very hard for people 'outside' the business community to understand the complexity of the issues, and the difficulties of corporate loyalty. Only those 'inside' can understand these pressures and appreciate when it is the right time to 'make a stand'. These, I believe, are the witnesses to Jesus in the business community in Australia, and they need our support.

Message

Dr Athol Gill of Whitley (Baptist) College, Melbourne, in his paper "Good News to the Rich"[3] expresses the basic message for this area of the community in expounding the story of Zacchaeus. He writes:

"When the people came out to be baptized by John and he called on them to bear fruits befitting repentance, he warned them not to bother claiming 'we have Abraham for our father ... for God is able from these stones to raise up children to Abraham.' (Luke 3:8). Those who full of enthusiasm want to be part of God's renewal movement in Israel, claiming the promises to Abraham, while not prepared to make an appropriate change of lifestyle, are no better off than the stones of the Judean wilderness. But a filthy rich tax-collector, whom everyone recognises as outside the pale, is declared to be a true son of Abraham as he repents, giving away half of his possessions and making appropriate reparation to all those whom he has oppressed. Salvation is his!

"You see, the Gospel is good news to the rich. In this story we are told that Jesus takes the initiative and extends the invitation. It is an invitation of grace which comes to Zaccheus while he was still a money-grubbing tax-collector. In the presence of Jesus, and in full view of everyone, the tax-collector makes the only appropriate response to the grace of God. He changes his way of living. Instead of living for himself and his money, he declares that from that moment onwards he will live for the poor and oppressed, and he demonstrates this in concrete actions. Jesus does not throw aside the drunk or the prostitute. He does not reject the rich oppressor. He opens the way of salvation for them and in His presence there is the power and the grace for them to change their way of living, to become truly children of Abraham. This is good news!"

As well, it is important for Christians to develop a theology of wealth which makes sense to those who are wealthy. Keith Suter[4] points out that money is in itself not seen as evil in the Bible, but part of God's creation. The evil arises from the love of money (1 Timothy 6). Suter explains John Wesley's principles on the use of money: Gain all you can by sensible lawful means; save all you can and refrain from unnecessary and wasteful expenditure; give all you can, after meeting household costs, to worthwhile causes.

He debates modern applications of the 18th Century observation on the cycle of debt and poverty:

Beggars make rags
Rags make paper
Paper makes money
Money makes banks
Banks make loans
Loans make debts
Debts make beggars
Beggars make rags.

So, at the heart of our evangelism in affluent secular societies, there needs to be a clear understanding of the interaction between faith and work; salvation and stewardship; poverty and wealth; charity and responsibility.

Effect

In a multicultural and liberal church, there is no difficulty justifying social action, but a certain timidity about its connection with evangelism. The strategies I have outlined are bringing these two Christian responsibilities together, in a way which is becoming interesting to many church people. Within the diverse Diocese of Melbourne, evangelicals tend to be into evangelism, and others tend to be into social action. Both streams are learning of the advantages of the other contribution: direct evangelism needs the credibility of caring in the community; and social action without the content of the Gospel is merely political action. There is now debate across the theological streams about how the two areas interact for mutual benefit.

The Melbourne community is never socially 'docile' but tends to be radically active in questioning the way society is going. The question is how we introduce credible evangelism into that participation.

There is a long tradition in Melbourne of individual ministers 'doing their own thing'. There is something of that in my own ministry in the areas described, but the danger is to become isolated in the process. Institutionally, our diocesan Department of Evangelism is now including within its programmes the development of pastoral care within the community, and social analysis of how the congregation relates to its neighbourhood. On the other side, church welfare agencies are examining how they can encourage more direct spiritual response to their caring ministries. So there is considerable movement in this area.

Discipleship and the Church

Current programmes which I know of from various churches are:

* a professional counselling programme from St James' Old Cathedral, in the western part of the City of Melbourne, designed to provide Christian counselling for office workers.
* a regular dialogue group between church leaders and the mining industry, controversial now because of environmental pressures.
* working relationships between some trade unions in Melbourne and the Anglican and Uniting Churches, particularly on industrial justice questions.
* a continuing strategy of dinners for political leaders.
* 'Ministers of Religion' are now compulsory members of all institutional ethics committees in Australia, in hospitals, universities, research institutes. Other Christians are there as community representatives, professionals etc.
* The Victorian State Government, in setting up community consultative groups, always includes at least one church representative if not three (Catholic, Uniting, Anglican).
* A Melbourne Christian businessmen's committee, of leading business figures, meets every Thursday for Bible study in the city, with others meeting for a Friday morning prayer breakfast, to work through how their spiritual beliefs work in the rough and tumble of the business world. A Christian

economists' group meets regularly in Sydney with contacts in Canberra and Melbourne for personal fellowship and support, but also to work through theological questions. They have contributed to the Oxford Conference on Faith and Economics.[5]

Resistance

Multicultural community creates a climate where people are conscious of Islam, Hinduism and Buddhism as being respectable Australian religions. This does not however seem to be saying that Christians cannot engage in evangelism. In fact, some indications of militant Islamic evangelism gives credibility to any Christian outreach.

There are no political or legal restrictions in Australia on direct evangelism, and indeed churches have access through 'statutory time' on radio and television to engaging in public evangelism.

But there is a less definable 'social climate' where evangelism must be discreet, non-discriminatory, non-accusatory, and where people engaging in evangelism need to establish their credibility by engaging seriously in community life. This is where social responsibility seems to me to be a gateway to effective evangelism.

Footnotes

1. *Where the River Flows* by Peter and Sue Kaldor (Lancer Books, Australia, 1988).
2. *Violence and Conflict Resolution* (Social Responsibilities Committee, Anglican Diocese of Melbourne, 1989).
3. *Australian Ministry Magazine* Issue 2/90.
4. *Asia Journal of Theology* October 1989.
5. The Conference papers and the statement "The Oxford Declaration on Christian Faith and Economics January 1990" produced by over 120 theologians, missiologists, businessmen and economists are published in *Tranformation* Vol 7, No 2, April 1990.

Chapter Seventeen

Gospel, Community and Church: Anglicans and the decade of evangelism

A report of the Theological Consultation held by The Evangelical Fellowship in the Anglican Communion at Kanamai Conference Centre, Mombasa, Kenya, April 17–22, 1990

Introduction

1. "This Conference, recognizing that evangelism is the primary task given to the Church, asks each Province and diocese of the Anglican Communion, in co-operation with other Christians, to make the closing years of this millenium a "Decade of Evangelism" with a renewed and united emphasis on making Christ known to the people of his world" (Lambeth Conference, 1988, Resolution 43).

2. In response to this Resolution, EFAC commissioned its Theological Resource Team to convene a study conference on the theology underlying the evangelism practised by evangelical Anglicans in different parts of the world. Thirteen Anglicans, bishops, presbyters, deaconesses, and lay men and women from Canada, Brazil, Kenya, Nigeria, India, United Kingdom, and U.S.A. met in Easter week. Our process of theology was to discuss and reflect in the light of Scripture on the following case-studies of evangelism:

– in nomadic communities in Kenya
– in rural Nigeria
– among Jewish People in the U.S.A.
– among the wealthy in Chile
– in a new suburban housing development in the United Kingdom
– among secular affluent people in Vancouver, Canada
– among decision makers in Melbourne, Australia

– among the displaced urban poor in Bangalore, India
– among the voiceless in South Africa
– among women in India
– in a mission diocese in North East Brazil
– in a new rural diocese in South Africa

3. Our report is limited by the extent of the case-studies we examined and the short time available. We do not pretend to offer a comprehensive survey or theology of every dimension of evangelism. From the examples studied, we attempt to draw out a fresh understanding of the Gospel and how to make it present among different communities. We invite others both to study our report, and where possible to do so in the light of the case studies underlying it. We especially invite them to enter into our experience by engaging in a similar process of reflection on particular models of evangelism that they know of. To facilitate this, we include the Guidelines which were used in the writing up of the case-studies for this consultation.

SECTION ONE: THE GOSPEL

4. The case-studies show examples of evangelism in widely different contexts around the world. They illustrate an almost bewildering array of the clothes the Gospel can wear. The word Gospel tends to be linked with many other adjectives or phrases which claim to define or qualify it. Some of these can be biblically endorsed; others are open to misunderstanding; some are falsifications of the Gospel. In the course of the case-studies and in the discussions which followed we noted examples of the following kinds of Gospel, referred to both positively and negatively:

Personal Gospel
Community Gospel
Two Covenant Gospel
Prosperity Gospel
Gospel with bias to the poor
Secular Gospel
Traditionalist Gospel
Male-hierarchical Gospel

Feminist Gospel
Political Gospel
Progressive Gospel
Social Gospel

Does this mean that there is a different Gospel for every context? Or that the Gospel is defined or discovered afresh in each context? In response to this we want to make three points: first that there is only one Gospel; second that the proclamation of that Gospel is clarified through conflict; third that every human context calls forth fresh understanding and perceived relevance of that one Gospel.

A. The Given-ness of the Gospel

5. The Gospel cannot be an ever changing thing because it is first of all a statement of something that has happened. It is objective, because it is rooted in historical events. These historical events include the action of God in the history of Israel, climaxing in the life, death and resurrection of Jesus of Nazareth. In these events God has acted for the salvation of humanity and the restoration of his whole creation. This is the essential Good News, and evangelism is essentially to make these events and their meaning known, with the accompanying summons to repentance, faith and obedience.

6. This is the reason why the Scriptures are the normative and authoritative source for evangelism. It is the Scriptures of both Testaments which are the primary witness to these events and provide the authoritative interpretation of them, in a way which no subsequent tradition or rational reflection can do. We reject, therefore, the tendency to treat Scripture as an equal partner with tradition and reason as alleged sources of authority. This is not the authentic Anglican position. The Scriptures give us both the authority *to* evangelise, (because they record the acts of God which he commands us to make known), and the authority *of* our evangelism (because they record the truth of the Gospel which God revealed through those acts).

B. Clarifying the Gospel

7. It is essentially the historical facts of what God has done in Christ that make the Gospel *Good* News. But it is only as it is proclaimed that it becomes Good *News*. The New Testament shows the process by which the Gospel as a proclaimed message was defined and clarified through confrontation. The affirmation that Jesus of Nazareth, crucified and risen, was the Messiah of Israel and the saviour of the world met resistance on two major fronts: from the Jewish religious establishment on the one hand, and from the dominant "secular" culture of the Greek-Roman world, on the other. Both of these conflicts resulted in significant defining of the Gospel. Both of them are also represented today, in the issue of evangelism in relation to Jews and in the conflict of the Gospel with the secular city of western civilization. Our case-studies and discussions reflected both of these, and it was clear that both fields of conflict compel us to clarify the Gospel in ways that are paradigmatic for other contexts, just as happened in the New Testament church.

i. "to the Jew first . . ."

8. Evangelism among the Jews throws into sharp focus, today as much as in the New Testament period, the claims for the uniqueness of Jesus, and is the test case for the legitimacy of evangelising people of any other faith.

9. The starting point of the apostolic Gospel was that Jesus of Nazareth was the Messiah. He was the one anointed by God to bring in the expected reign of God which would fulfil God's purpose for creation, his promises to Israel, and his goal of redemption for the nations.

10. Jesus must not be cut off from his historical and scriptural roots, as some forms of religious pluralism do by regarding him as merely one among several great founders of new religions. But the New Testament itself begins by introducing Jesus as the "son of Abraham and son of David", the completion of a particular history which led up to him and found its goal and fulfilment in his arrival. His uniqueness is therefore integrally tied to the uniqueness of Israel. They were unique in being the ones chosen

by God to be the recipients of his revelation and the vehicles of his saving purpose for the nations. And their uniqueness was in turn integrally tied to the uniqueness of Yahweh as God (e.g. Deut. 4:32ff., Isa. 43:8-13, etc).

11. The importance, therefore, of the Jewish roots of the Christian faith is that it not only grounds the Gospel in specific history, but also that the uniqueness of both Israel and Yahweh flow together into the uniqueness of Jesus, the Messiah, who embodied the one and incarnated the other. On both counts the Christian Gospel resists the relativizing reduction of Jesus purveyed by religious pluralism.

12. The expectation of the Hebrew Bible, and of Jews at the time of Jesus, was that the coming of the Messiah would signal first the restoration of Israel and then the ingathering of the nations to the final, redeemed people of God. The good news would be preached first to "the lost sheep of Israel" and then "to the ends of the earth". But both were part of the one eschatological scenario at the close of the age. This understanding lies behind Paul's theology and practice of mission (which was endorsed by the rest of the apostles, Acts 15:12–18), in going first to the Jews but also stressing the eschatological significance of the Gentile mission. The importance of this for the theology of evangelism is that Jesus is the saviour of the world *because* he is the Messiah of Israel. He cannot be one and not the other. If he is not the Messiah for the Jews, then he cannot be saviour for the Gentiles. If evangelism among Jews is disallowed, it cuts the nerve of all other evangelism.

13. This is built into the structure of the covenant with Abraham itself. The Jews exist, as the people of God, only in order that the blessing of Abraham should come to all nations. That was their uniqueness in God's universal redemptive purpose. The Gospel therefore has to be Good News for the Jews if it is to be Good News for anyone else. Jesus is unique for the Jews, because the Jews were unique for the sake of the Gentiles.

14. At the heart of the New Testament Gospel is the reconciliation of Jew and Gentile as one new person in the Messiah, Jesus (Eph. 2:11–3:6, Gal. 3:28). By contrast, the so-called "Two

Covenant Theory" not only fails to bring about this reconciliation and oneness (and on that score alone must be a false gospel), but is also used by some as a way of keeping Christians from the duty of presenting to the Jewish community the challenge of the claims of Jesus to be the Messiah and to be reconciled to God through him. For this reason, although it is a theory of Christian origin, it has been welcomed by some Jews in the U.S.A. as a means of neutralizing Christian evangelism in their midst.

15. Reconciliation includes making peace, through Christ the Prince of Peace. Peace, biblically, is the fruit of justice, and both are prominent in the prophetic vision of the Messiah's ministry in the Old Testament. The proclamation of the Gospel, therefore, in any community cannot be separated from the moral demand of God for justice within and between communities. The question of whether the return of the Jews to the land of Palestine in this century is to be regarded as the fulfilment of biblical prophecy was not one our consultation wished to answer. But we would affirm that, whatever view one takes on that disputed issue it cannot be used to short-circuit the concern for justice which is indisputably biblical and prophetic. The presentation of the claims of Jesus as Messiah among the Jews should not be isolated from a deeper awareness of God's desire for justice and peace among all the present inhabitants of the land of Israel.

ii) ". . . and also to the Greek"

16. When the Gospel confronts the secular city, it is like the rock in the dream of Nebuchadnezzar in Daniel 2. It comes from outside, "not made with human hands", and it faces the statue of human kingdoms with the inevitability of its own shattering fall.

17. The secular city is a declaration of humanity's independence from God. In the city people can be anonymous, immoral, lustful and dishonest. It is a place where man is God: a counter-creation because of dissatisfaction with God's creation, the place whose origin was the restlessness of Cain fleeing from God's presence.

18. Into this city comes the Word of God. Its effect is confounding, because the Word of God does what the city

constitutionally denies. It says, "There is another reality", to people caught up in the myth that the city is the only reality (Isa. 47:7f.). All the city can do with Jesus Christ is to crucify him, because he challenges its idolatry with a reality that the city cannot handle and survive. Therefore, in the city, evangelism has to begin from the resurrection, a new reality, a new beginning, a new creation.

19. In the city, the Gospel is focused and refined in conflict with militant secularism just as much as it is in the conflicts with other militant ideologies and religions. Christians in the city need to be aware of this conflictual dimension to their witness. Secularism forces us to clarify the Gospel by showing that it is first a word of judgement ("We preach Christ crucified" was said in Corinth), but also that it injects a hope (the resurrection) which cannot be found in the city itself. The Gospel is an objective reality which challenges and contradicts the wisdom of the age (the root meaning of "secular"). But its apparent foolishness and weakness to the secular mind conceals its true nature as the power of God for salvation (1 Cor. 1:18–2:5). The Gospel calls the city to account and to change in order to conform with it. Evangelism in the city must never become a matter of trying to make the Gospel fit in with and conform to the city's constricted and idolatrous view of reality.

20. Secularism has bred relativism, the view that the only truth is that there is no ultimate truth. Relativism, the companion of pluralism, can only cope with the Word of God by reducing it to a word from a god which can be conveniently marginalized. It can thus subvert or neutralize the uncomfortable challenge of the Gospel by treating it as just one view among many, the private fantasy of just one religious group. Those who evangelize are dismissed as arrogant and intolerant for claiming to know and propagate what they claim to be the truth.

21. Our reponse to this must be that evangelism is not an arrogant or patronising claim that *"We have the Gospel,* and we are going to share it with you", but rather, *"There is a Gospel,* and all of us together stand under it, facing its judgement as well as its promise". We do not own the Gospel. We are confronted by

it, as everyone is. And we are entrusted with it as heralds who take no credit for inventing it but bear the responsibility of announcing it.

C. One Gospel: Many clothes

22. Once we have accepted the objective givenness of the Gospel, and seen its message sharpened and refined through confrontation, we can go on to see how at the same time *any* human context potentially enriches our understanding of how the Gospel is Good News for creation and humanity. The richness of the case studies brought home to us afresh this multi-faceted nature of the Gospel diamond. Each context that we looked at highlighted fresh facets of the whole spectrum of biblical teaching. The theology that undergirds our evangelism has to be broad enough therefore to incorporate all these facets. Some which shone through repeatedly were: the wholeness of creation; the image of God in humanity; the dignity of every person, man and woman; the importance of human community; the personal and collective sinfulness of idolatry, oppression, inequality, greed and all that spoils human life as God desires it; the power of God to transform both individual persons and whole communities through Christ.

23. *There is* Good News for the individual, for the family, for the community, for the nomad, for the commuter, for the oppressed, for the sick, for the poor, for the wicked, for the sinner and the sinned against. In every case it will be Good News *in Christ*, and based on the irreducible historical facts and their apostolic interpretation. We cannot change the facts and we are not at liberty to change the authoritative interpretation of them in Scripture in an attempt to make the Gospel somehow more congenial to any age or culture. To that degree, the process of contextualization must be uncompromising as regards that givenness. We do not discover the Gospel afresh in every new context, nor does the context define the Gospel. At the same time, however, our faithfulness as stewards of the Gospel requires us to understand and express the Gospel in ways that relate effectively to every context, affirming what is good and challenging what is evil. The process of contextualization

therefore must also be open to all that the infinite variety of historical, geographical, and social contexts calls forth from the Gospel as the power of God for salvation and the first-fruits of a new creation.

SECTION TWO: THE COMMUNITY

A. Evangelizing Communities

24. God created humanity to live as persons in community. A community is a cohesive group of persons in a given area that has a sense of belonging and is bonded together by a common culture, language, religion, interests, customs, traditions, etc. Most communities of this nature are found in rural areas and also in cities pocketed in the oldest sections and in temporary fringe settlements.

25. We need to use every branch of knowledge and the tools of the social sciences in understanding communities. Often the poor have a stronger sense of community than the rich who tend to be more deprived and isolated: "poor areas have smaller walls; the rich haver higher walls to break down." Sometimes we may need to arouse the political consciousness of a community by asking the question why they are living in that particular community as opposed to another, when the goal is often to escape from the community as circumstances improve.

26. Jesus Christ emptied himself and came to live within a particular human community. The evangelist must also go and live among the people he seeks to evangelize, sharing the gospel and the presence of Jesus Christ in that way. As Jesus lived in the midst of others and as he travelled between village and city, he saw the groups who were harassed and helpless looking "like sheep without a shepherd" and sought to deal with that harassment and helplessness. An incarnational approach to mission enables one to see the things that need to be done and then discern how and where to take action. We need to rediscover the total possibility of Christ and the Gospel for the total needs of people.

27. We recommend, therefore, that where a recognizable community exists the approach of the Gospel should be a community approach. It should not be imposed on the community but should demonstrate, like Jesus, the ability to meet people where they are. There should be respect for the uniqueness of a particular community. Where there are closely knit cohesive communities we should try to communicate the Gospel to the whole community and its kinship network rather than only to the individual.

28. This is illustrated in the case study of the strategy used by the Diocese of Mount Kenya East towards the Gabbra community. A model and inspiration for this strategy was found in the work of the Roman Catholic Church through Father Vincent Donovan in Northern Tanzania (which in itself shows the value of learning from another Christian tradition). Father Donovan had changed from a strategy which had focused on the individual ("luring the children into Christian schools") because it had resulted in extracting them from their community and had thus failed to reach the community as a whole. Instead he chose to share the life of the whole community and to teach the Christian faith to all. This gave the whole community the opportunity to articulate the Gospel for themselves and then to respond corporately to the Gospel through their leader/chief. It was not a case of the community simply following the lead of the chief, but of him expressing for all the result of their community discussion and decision.

29. Community evangelism and individual evangelism must be complementary. Neither renders the other unnecessary. Any community orientated evangelism which fails to present the need for individual response to God in repentance and faith falls short of the biblical view of personal accountability to God as part of our essential humanity. When a community responds there is also the need to develop individual allegiance and commitment, so that that response is constantly confirmed and renewed personally and corporately. Likewise, however, any individual evangelism which fails to include the challenge of commitment to the Christian community and to the task of permeating the wider human community with Christian salt and light falls short of the biblical view of God's will for human life in relationship.

Individual conversion must be earthed in a new commitment to family, neighbourhood, wider society, and the worlds of work and leisure.

30. This concern for communities is not based on a naive assumption that community is in and of itself necessarily a good thing. In a fallen world it is clear that human beings can form communities for evil purposes. Some communities only exist by the exclusion of others from rights and privileges. Others find their own group identity by the defining and diminishing of others. "Building community" is not therefore to be confused with merely bolstering corporate structures that embody evil, pride or injustice. The work of breaking down as well as building up is part of the prophetic ministry in relation to fallen human communities. Anglicans are sometimes invited to give a religious sanction to certain kinds of community (e.g by chaplaincy) when in some cases the work of evangelism should challenge the objectives, methods or even the very existence of such communities.

B. Rich and Poor

31. God is fair and is no respecter of persons. When his fairness encounters the unfairness of human society to restore righteousness and justice it necessarily appears to be 'biased' in favour of righteousness and against injustice. However, his fairness does not place any barriers to people of any economic position, poor or rich. The expression 'God's bias to the poor', therefore, is not to attribute favouritism or partiality to God. Rather it describes the outworking of his impartiality on behalf of those who are the victims of human partiality and injustice. Furthermore, to say that God has a 'bias to the poor', rightly understood, by no means excludes his love towards the rich. While he longs to see the poor rescued and relieved, he also longs to see the rich liberated from slavery to wealth, from their anxiety and spiritual blindness. These two processes are linked. For in Jesus' ministry and in our response to the Gospel the poor are not just 'another group'. It is the preaching of Good News to the poor and the way the poor respond to it which indicate the way in which the Good News is to be understood, received and responded to by all.

32. All economic systems must be judged by Christian values. We commend the following summary of the findings from the Oxford Conference on Christian Faith and Economics:

"Economic systems must be judged by their ability both to create wealth and to distribute it justly. Both freedom rights and sustenance rights are important and are grounded not in societal fiat but in God's creation of persons in the divine image. The God of the Bible demands special attention to the weak, especially poor members of the community, because of their vulnerability; in this sense justice is biased. But civil arrangements rendering justice dare not go beyond what is due to the poor or rich; in that sense justice is ultimately impartial. Biblical values and historical experience call Christians to work for democracy while recognising that racism, materialism and concentrated economic power often lead democracies to marginalise the poor and act unjustly."

33. We note that a significant stumbling block to evangelistic integrity is the fact that in contemporary societies evangelicals are found to be more often allied to the capitalist system and trying merely to humanise it. There is a need therefore to be aware of the sinfulness of capitalism, to realise that it is transitory, to be willing to consider alternatives and to seek to replace it with a system that is more in line with God's will. This is not a naive faith that any alternative will be perfect. It is recognized that whatever replaces it will have its own shortcomings concerning which our grandchildren in their turn will need to exercise discrimination. Nevertheless evangelistic credibility in each generation must involve rejection of whatever unholy alliances with mammon constitute the current dominant idolatry.

34. It was the testimony of those whose calling is to work pastorally and evangelistically among the rich that the faithful and Christlike exercise of such a ministry can be painful and demanding. At the heart of our evangelism in affluent settled societies, there needs to be a clear understanding of the interaction between faith and work; salvation and stewardship; poverty and wealth; charity and responsibility. We noted the importance of the 'Zacchaeus principle': that is, looking for those who are open to change and giving them the opportunity to

define for themselves the terms in which that change is to be expressed. The difference between Zaccheus and the rich young ruler was that the rich young ruler was not open to change; therefore Jesus defined the terms for him, which he rejected. It is important to hold before those wealthy people who turn to Christ the scope and opportunity of discovering the terms that Jesus would set before them in relation to the poor, rather than exposing them to those who would just seek their money. We need to bring people to the Cross to say: "Do whatever you like with me." The way people are changed is part of the message of the Gospel. The materially changed lives, values and priorities of those who respond to the claims and challenge of Christ must be signs of the Word that is preached.

35. Reflecting on the relationship between wealthy and poor Christians we drew on the example of the Apostle Paul. While engaging in mission to the Gentiles, Paul also challenged the Church in Jerusalem to recognise reciprocity of blessing whereby the Gentiles received from the spiritual heritage of the Jews through Jesus and the Jewish Christians received material blessing from Gentile churches (Rom. 15:26f.). Paul called this process *koinonia*, partnership in the Gospel and obedience to the Gospel (2 Cor.8:13–15, 9:12ff., Phil. 4:15–18). It was a proof of the authenticity of his evangelistic ministry and its success depended on Paul's personal and theological credibility with both givers and receivers.

36. There is a great need for such partnership today through reciprocal sharing whereby we can benefit from one another. The African Church, for example, is growing remarkably and has much spiritual, liturgical and theological wealth to share. This can be contributed as Two Thirds World personnel come to share in the evangelization of the West, and are explicitly invited to do so.

37. At the same time, however, people observe that the economies of many African countries, including those with rapid Christian growth, are facing severe problems. An important question arises, therefore, as to how this success in winning people to Christ relates to combatting poverty. As stewards of God's resources, our partnership must extend to sharing skills

and resources which God has given for the benefit of all, not only to extend his kingdom evangelistically but also to combat the sufferings and evils of poverty.

38. All of us are affected by our own cultural settings in the way we read Scripture. The poor and the rich alike can try to evolve a theological rationale to protect their positions and interests. It is not possible to be objective from our own position alone. We need the constant challenge and interaction from those in other cultural contexts. However we should be aware that while it may be easy, from a distance, to identify a clear cut issue in a particular context which the church there should address (such as racialism, materialism or poverty), for those involved in the issue, the starting place of their evangelistic engagement "where people are" often involves a degree of compromise. Here we have to reflect on the balance and tension in Jesus' own ministry in the midst of similar divisive issues. We can observe, on the one hand, his meals and social intercourse with national traitors (tax-collectors), prostitutes, and others who scandalised the society, and, on the other hand the fact that he associated with those who were among the oppressors of the society – Romans, Sadducees and a ruler of the Jews (Nicodemus).

C. Women

39. Our reflection on evangelism by women and among women identified several special needs to which the church must give attention. In many societies today women are unable to experience or express the dignity and worth which the Bible affirms for them as being made in the image of God alongside men and joint heirs in Christ with men. Women's basic need is to recognise their own sense of worth, a sense of being needed, included and valued. Men need to acknowledge it and women need to believe it. Above all, women need to be assured again of their identity in Christ, which is the restoration of their full and equal humanity.

40. Women need to move from living reactively to the pressures of others upon them to choosing to live in response to God's purpose for them. This means a fuller awareness of the Holy

Spirit and his gifts in them through Christ which empower them to make their authentic contribution to the community. In India for example, many women are burdened with cultural inhibitions and natural timidity. In many situations women are oppressed but that oppression manifests itself in different ways with different effects in different contexts. In all situations the proclamation of God's unchanging good news in Jesus Christ will be given by women and for women in a way that responds to the various realities in which they find themselves. In all situations women will need to be enabled to take up their responsibilities and encouraged to develop their God-given gifts for the building up of the family, the church and in the extension of His Kingdom. It is recognised that in some societies only women can evangelize women.

41. Women commonly function at a deeper emotional level than men and need each other in order to build up something that has been destroyed inside them. If the Christian community provides a sense of belonging it becomes a place where the woman not only recovers something which she has lost but also rediscovers the identity and freedom which enable her to reach out to help and renew others.

D. The New Community

42. Jesus created a new community among his own disciples, and after his resurrection they extended his principle into the community life of the early church (Acts 2 and 4). There is a distinctive flavour to the Christian community, focused on allegiance to the Lord, Bible reading, worship, sacraments, fellowship and prayer, which should enable it to be a service to and a leaven in the wider community in which it is set. There is no new humanity if there are not first of all new persons renewed by baptism and the Holy Spirit, living according to the Gospel of the kingdom of God. The purpose of evangelization is precisely this interior change.

43. Where there is no deep sense of community, as in an urban area, then the task of the church is to recreate communities. The local church is the renewed community in Christ. The church

which has ceased to be a community is dead. The biggest challenge to the church in areas where community cohesiveness has broken down is to create new communities which can provide a sense of belonging and concern in our complex and secular society. The Christian home should be the most visible manifestation of the church in the community. For this reason, evangelistic strategy needs to put a high priority on the establishment and spiritual nurture of Christian homes.

44. Creating and recreating a community is inherent in the Anglican approach through its commitment to territoriality (parish, diocese and province) and catholicity. The Decade of Evangelism is not just a matter of harnessing Anglicans and Anglicanism to someone else's franchised form of evangelism. If at all possible, the lukewarm, tradition-bound community can be renewed from within in preference to creating a new community. For example old church structures can be renewed by the implementation of proven movements from other parts of the Christian communion, such as, for example, the "cursillo" movement of holding teaching retreats on Christian doctrine and ethics, and other lay training schemes.

45. A particular bridge between the life of the Christian community and the wider community is when the Church celebrates life-changing events in baptisms, confirmations, weddings and funerals. These events draw in many nominal or non-Christians and thus have evangelistic potential as times when people can be moved to action. For example, at services of adult baptism and confirmation, there can be a sensitive proclamation of the Gospel with an invitation to join those being baptized; at a wedding there can be an opportunity for renewing of marriage vows for those who come as guests; and at a funeral there is the opportunity for sensitive appeal to face and prepare for the inevitability of death.

SECTION THREE:
WAYS FORWARD FOR THE CHURCH

A. Preparation

46. It is important that in engaging in the Decade of Evangelism, Anglicans attend to their spiritual health and are sure of their identity in Jesus Christ. Nigerian Anglicans held a bishop's retreat recently on the theme Purity and Power. It is important that we are purified so that what we proclaim is not negated by our lives. Syncretism, for example, is a major problem for us all. We often try and divide our lives, giving part of it to Christ and part of it to something else, be it another faith or materialism. In some situations the Church has become preoccupied with maintenance rather than with mission, internal politics rather than God's love for the world. We must begin with the glory of God and seek a fresh vision of his will and purpose for the Church in each community.

47. A strength of the Anglican approach is our integration with the community and the sense of territorial responsibility expressed in pastoral care for dioceses and parishes. We are charged to be committed to and involved with the communities in which we are set. Conversely, a common weakness is that we often compromise by adopting uncritically that community's values and thereby adulterate and discredit the Gospel.

48. In order to avoid this danger, we need to recognize the tension in the prime biblical model of evangelism which is incarnational. In no way do we want to be less involved with our communities but we want to follow the distinctiveness of Christ and be in the world but not of it. Often we are afraid of being different and simply acquiesce in the values of the community. One of the great services we offer each other as an international communion is to offer loving and constructive critique of each other's evangelistic response to our situations. This process took place intensively at the Lambeth Conference where brother bishops were able to help each other appraise their own situations afresh. This process enables us to look at ourselves critically and realize that though what we are doing is not unscriptural, there may be a better way.

49. For example, the Two-Thirds World Church views with perplexity the western Church's marriage with power and materialism. It applauds the concern with which the western Church seeks to start where western people are. But it longs to see a more faithful application of the 'Zaccheus principle' whereby Christian disciples identify with the aspirations of the poor. This would facilitate a powerful witness to the world and a necessary partnership with the Church in the Two-Thirds World in combatting poverty.

50. As further examples: African church leaders are perplexed by the excessive authority and deference given to them in their societies and have been helped by brethren in other parts of the world to see a more servant-style of leadership. African church leaders have helped western Christians to see the way in which it is necessary to ask governments of Muslim countries to extend the same freedoms to religious minorities as Muslim communities ask for in western democracries.

B. The Sacraments.

51. At the heart of our worship are the sacraments of the Gospel events through which God entered the world as it is, to transform and redeem it by his presence, and by which we are identified with the death and resurrection of Jesus Christ. Because of God's commitment to us we die to self and live for his service. We, like his body, must be broken in order to be shared. Christians caught up in the values of our cultures, such as materialism, individualism and authoritarianism, must continually be broken in order that the life of God may be shared. God's love is only owned as it is given away. (2 Cor. 2:14ff).

52. There is thus a sacramental aspect to the incarnational presence and evangelism of the people of God. What is of the creation is taken, broken, transformed and shared as bearers of the life of God. However, it is a distortion of this to regard participation in the sacraments alone as an adequate expression of Christian commitment or to suggest that evangelism is unnecessary in a context where a large proportion of the population has been baptized.

53. In communities where outsiders to the Church request baptism for their children, clear doctrine and wise pastoral judgement is required. The very request represents a positive step to be encouraged rather than quenched. Where an "open" policy is deemed appropriate, such a degree of acceptance only makes sense when it is accompanied by a clear presentation of the Gospel which parents can understand and articulate for themselves and say they have accepted. Operated with integrity, this open approach can have great evangelistic potential. On the other hand, some churches adopt a rigorously strict policy which closes the door to most outside requests for baptism, and the reasons for this are equally well understood. However, such a policy not only confirms some people's prejudices about the church but also seems to punish people who are victims of a secular world view which they have absorbed from the surrounding culture without much personal responsibility for it. They should not be the targets of our righteous anger with secularism or our frustrations with folk religion at the point when they make even a minimal movement towards God. Jesus had severe and trenchant words for people who perpetuated the dominant world-view in his society, but had loving words for those caught up in it who turned to him even in their confusion. Secularism and residual folk religion must of course be challenged and their inadequacy exposed. But the place to do it is the continuous teaching of scripture and the use of every medium of engagement in the public arena.

C. Varieties of Context

54. Whatever the situation, the Church is called to envisage and express the kingdom of God. This entails the exhilarating exercise of imagining how the community may be transformed, and locating the key issues to be addressed. The case studies provided many examples of this.

In Melbourne, Australia, Christians and others in decision-making roles meet to understand and sift the values underlying issues of business, politics, industry and medicine.

In Bangalore, India a church acts as an advocate in solidarity with displaced slum-dwellers to ensure that government services are provided swiftly.

In Woking, England, a church cries out against the blasphemy of housing estates without community facilities or places of worship.

In Nigeria, a diocese works with rural communities to provide water supplies and improve their harvests by organising co-operatives.

In Brazil, parishes create day-care centres for the children of poor working women, clubs for unemployed mothers, and retirement clubs for lonely old people in the slums.

In Vancouver the culture is now so completely secularised that the Word of God can only be presented in starkest contrast to the values of that society. Here Christians must take heart that their Gospel will be refined and focused in conflict with rampant secularism just as the faith of other Christians has been refined and focused in conflict with other militant ideologies and religions.

55. In these diverse situations, the common thread is the will of God that people in community should live in circumstances of peace, sufficiency and justice and that every person should experience salvation and wholeness in Christ. So the Church as the community of faith within the wider community both bears the vision and acts as a catalyst in making that vision a reality. A Christian project or initiative, however small – a hospitable home, a playgroup, a language class – can be a sign of what society under God can be, and every new believer can be a sign of the new humanity in Christ.

D. The Local Church and Lay Ministries.

56. The local church is the best agent of evangelism. Evangelism takes place as people who are being changed by the Gospel share their new life in Christ. Church members are themselves the most eloquent testimony (whether good or bad) of the word that is preached (2 Cor. 3:2f.). Therefore it is vital that church members be enlisted, trained and commissioned into ministry. It is the lay people who are in the front line of evangelism, albeit trained and supported by the clergy, and directed by the bishop. Indeed the bishop has a unique opportunity to demonstrate the priority of evangelism in his own ministry. A Nigerian bishop

engages in training and visiting with lay evangelistic teams from time to time. The lay people motivated and mobilised in this way became enthusiastic and effective evangelists.

57. Most urgent of all is for the church to recognise and encourage Christian women as full partners with men in evangelism and mission. The God-given gifts, talents, and abilities of women should be recognised by the church. In too many situations the Church mirrors society in denying the dignity and worth of women and suppressing their gifts and concerns. This is contrary to scripture's teaching on the created equality of the sexes and the priesthood of all believers. In one African diocese, where two-thirds of the church members are women, all the boards, committees, and decision-making positions are filled by men.

58. We are not commending an aggressive, strident feminism. Nor is our concern necessarily related to the ordination of women. In some cases ordination can be a crippling of actual ministry (for men or women). Our concern is with the mobilization of the whole of God's people for evangelism. The implications for evangelism are grave if we ignore so high a percentage of our work-force. There is an added seriousness when we realise that there are many ministries best suited to the characteristic courage and sensitivity of women, and some situations which, of their very nature, can only be tackled by women.

59. What we have said about women is, to some extent, true of the Church's youth. They too have a unique part to play as evangelists to their peers and elders. We were meeting on the same site as young Kenyans training for and engaging in evangelism among Muslims. We were greatly impressed and encouraged by their commitment and enthusiasm. In Nigeria too, we were told, it is the young people who have the idealism, energy and zeal to engage in sacrificial and time-consuming evangelism.

60. Having stressed the responsibility of all church members in evangelism, we recognize also the specialist ministry of those with the particular gift of evangelism. However, there is a great

lack of such specialist evangelists and even where they are in evidence, they are given a decidedly low status. There is a major need for the selection, training and commissioning of those with this gift. The importance of their ministry should be recognised by salary levels equivalent to the clergy.

CONCLUSION

61. Evangelism is God's work and can only be carried out at his call, in his strength and with the resources he provides. According to his promise he has given his Holy Spirit to his Church, so that every member can be a witness (Acts 1:8). Today, as at the first Pentecost, we believe the Spirit is poured out on all God's people, without distinction of sex, age, status, race or education (Acts 2:17–18; 4:13). This means that we can approach mission even in difficult areas with hope and faith. A bishop in a desperately needy situation in South Africa writes: "The diocese can never be rich, but we believe that there are sufficient human and material resources within it to do the work that God has brought it into existence to do". There is a liberty in being able to say "We can only do what God gives us leaders and resources to do". This instance can be multiplied many times around the world, wherever churches, while engaged in mutual responsibility and interdependence, still rely on God's provision for their growth and propagation.

62. The evangelistic methods and training of parachurch agencies are a welcome resource for Anglicans when they are soundly based in scripture and appropriate to the local setting. However, we would maintain that the Anglican church has a very distinctive contribution to make to evangelism, through its long term, indigenous ministry to a community. While it is easy to be envious or discouraged by the success of fast-growing sects, or the apparent impact of emotional mass evangelism, we believe that our Anglican tradition of balanced biblical teaching and authorised church planting as an evangelistic method best serves the spiritual, pastoral and organisational needs of God's people, and has a positive record of lasting evangelistic fruitfulness. It is our prayer that the Decade of Evangelism will energise us to learn from and correct our failings and to do better what we already do well.

A Selective Bibliography and Resource List on Integral Evangelism

This bibliography is selected from the writings and work of Christian mission theologians from Africa, Asia and Latin America and from contexts of poverty and religious pluralism. It is in these contexts that wholistic evangelism has emerged. This material gives first hand access to practical situations and examples of wholistic evangelism.

Books and Articles

1. *Proclaiming Christ in Christ's Way* edited by Vinay Samuel and Albrecht Hauser (Oxford, Regnum, 1989) contains The Stuttgart Statement on Evangelism produced by evangelicals in the WCC
Also
"Evangelicals and Wholistic Evangelism" Chris Sugden
"World Evangelisation, Institutional Evangelicalism and the Future of Christian World Mission" Kwame Bediako
"Gospel and Culture" Vinay Samuel
"Christians in Plural Societies" Michael Nazir Ali
"Evangelisation and Culture" David Gitari (Lambeth Lecture)
"Christian Ethics and the Good News of the Kingdom" Ron Sider
"Evangelising a Secular Society – Europe" Raymond Fung
"Communicating in Music" Per Harling
"Christian Marxist Dialogue" Peter Kuzmic
"The Politics of the Kingdom of God and the Political Mission of the Church" Rene Padilla
"Is Dr King on Board" William Pannell

2. *Social Concern and Evangelisation*
   i. The January 1990 issue of *Transformation* (P.O. Box 70, Oxford) contains material from the Social Concern and Evangelisation Track at Lausanne II Manila 1989
"Good News to the Poor" Tom Houston
"Social Concern and Evangelisation" Vinay Samuel

"What does the Gospel have to say to disabled persons?" Joni Eareckson Tada
"Reaching the Oppressed" Caesar Molebatsi (South Africa)
"Voicelessness" Moss Nthla (South Africa)
"Evangelicals and Racism – The Lausanne II Press Conference with Caesar Molebatsi, Michael Cassidy and Nico Smith (South Africa) and Vinay Samuel (India)

ii. The July 1990 issue of *Transformation* contains the following:
"The report of the Social Concern Track"
"Guidelines for case-studies" by C.B. Samuel. These guidelines are to enable people to record, reflect on and evaluate evangelism in practice. They have been widely used around the world and in the U.K. also.
"The Kingdom Manifesto" – a document from the Evangelical Fellowship of New Zealand giving a biblical base for wholistic evangelism.

iii. "The Living God in Contemporary Life" – a statement from mission theologians from the Two-Thirds World on The Living God and Human Cultures, Idolatry Today, the Incarnation, History and Structures. In *Transformation* April 1988.

3. *Evangelical Witness in South Africa* – a critique of Evangelical Theology and Practice by South African Evangelicals. An important discussion of relevant and irrelevant evangelism in the South African context. In *Transformation* January 1987 and also published by the Evangelical Alliance, 186 Kennington Park Road, London SE11, U.K.

4. *Mission and Evangelism – an Ecumenical Affirmation* (Geneva, W.C.C.) An excellent statement on mission, the W.C.C.'s best selling publication.

5. Orlando Costas *The Integrity of Mission – The Inner Life and Outreach of the Church* (Harper and Row, 1979)

6. Michael Nazir-Ali *Frontiers in Muslim-Christian Encounter* (Oxford, Regnum, 1987) includes articles on
"The Gospel's offer of wholeness"
"Evangelization – a profile"
"Christianity in relation to other faiths"
"Wholeness and Fragmentation – the Gospel and Repression"

7. Ray Bakke *The Urban Christian* (MARC Europe and Kingsway). A summary of insightful and important material on urban mission.

8. *Sharing Jesus in the Two Thirds World* edited by Vinay Samuel and Chris Sugden (Eerdmans/Regnum, 1984) contains
"Proclaiming Christ in the Two Thirds World" Orlando Costas
"Christology and Mission in the Two Thirds World" Rene Padilla
"The Liberating Options of Jesus" Norberto Saracco
"Biblical Christologies in the Context of African Traditional Religions" Kwame Bediako

"Christology in the Life and Religion of the Balinese" Wayan Mastra
"Biblical Christianity in the Context of Buddhism" David Lim
"Significant Trends in Christology in Western Scholarly Debate" David Cook

9. *Transformation – The Church in Response to Human Need* A report of an international consultation on development with study questions for churches. (Nottingham, Grove Booklets, 1986)

10. *Jesus and Social Ethics* by Stephen Mott (Grove Books, Nottingham, 1984). A seminal study on the social significance of the ministry of Jesus, especially in confronting the status differentials of his society.

Video Material

1. *Seeing People through the eyes of Jesus* – 12 minute video of 3 case studies from India, Peru and Kenya, available from Scripture Union, 130 City Road, London EC1

2. *To Canterbury with a Camel* – the story of evangelism in the Diocese of Mount Kenya East available from CMS, 157 Waterloo Road, London SE1

3. *Crossing Cultures* – evangelism across cultures with John Wallis, Vinay Samuel, Chris Sugden, Art Beales (USA) available from BMMF Interserve, Whitefield House, 186 Kennington Park Road, London SE 11 4BT

Training Courses

The Gospel to the Whole Person – A Course in Evangelism to Communities A study action guide based on the WCC *Mission and Evangelism* statement which focuses on researching a people-group in their religious, social, economic and political context and developing strategies for addressing the good news to their total situation. Published by The Association for Theological Education by Extension, P.O.520, 13 Hutchins Road, Cooke Town, Bangalore, 560005, India. The course consists of a 10 week programme, with 4 one hour study units a week and one tutorial group meeting a week.

Contributors and Participants

The Rev. Professor Robinson Cavalcanti is dean of political science at the University of Kamamboko, Brazil and secretary of EFAC Brazil.

The Rev. Alfred Cooper is pastor of a church in Santiago, Chile.

Rt. Rev. David Evans, formerly Bishop of Peru, is assistant bishop of Bradford in the Church of England and EFAC's international co-ordinator.

Rt. Rev. Emmanuel Gbonigi is Bishop of Akure, Nigeria and president of EFAC Nigeria.

Rt. Rev. Dr. David Gitari is Bishop of Kerugoya, Kenya and East African Secretary of EFAC.

The Rev. Julius Kalu is Principal of the Christian Industrial Training Centre, Mombasa, Kenya.

The Rev. Andrew Knowles is vicar of St. Andrew's Church, Goldsworth Park, Woking, England.

Rt. Rev. Philip Le Feuvre is Bishop of the Diocese of St. Mark the Evangelist, South Africa.

The Rev. Samson Mwaluda is Principal of the Coast Bible College, Mombasa, Kenya.

Mrs. Simcha Newton is studying at Trinity Episcopal School for Ministry, Ambridge, Pennsylvania, U.S.A.

The Ven. Alan Nichols is Archdeacon of Melbourne, Australia.

The Rev. Henry Paltridge is lecturer at Coast Bible College, Mombasa, Kenya.

Mrs. Fran Robinson is a pastoral counsellor in Vancouver, Canada.

Canon Harry Robinson is Rector of St. John's Church (Shaughnessy) Vancouver, Canada.

Canon Dr. Vinay Samuel, formerly general secretary of EFAC, is a pastor of a C.S.I. Hindustani congregation in Bangalore, South India.

Rev. Dr. John Stott is president of Christian Impact, London, and founder and past president of EFAC.

Rev. Dr. Christopher Sugden is registrar and director of the Oxford Centre for Mission Studies, England, and managing editor of the EFAC Bulletin.

Mrs. Juliet Thomas is Co-ordinator of Women's Ministries, Operation Mobilisation, Bangalore, India.

Dss. Pamela Wilding is Director of Secretarial Studies at St. Andrew's Institute for Mission and Evangelism, Kerugoya, Kenya.

Rev. Dr. Christopher Wright is director of studies at All Nations Christian College, Easneye, Ware, England and co-ordinator of the EFAC Theological Resource Team.